1 MONTH OF FREE READING

at
www.ForgottenBooks.com

By purchasing this book you are eligible for one month membership to ForgottenBooks.com, giving you unlimited access to our entire collection of over 1,000,000 titles via our web site and mobile apps.

To claim your free month visit:
www.forgottenbooks.com/free788140

* Offer is valid for 45 days from date of purchase. Terms and conditions apply.

ISBN 978-0-483-55205-0
PIBN 10788140

This book is a reproduction of an important historical work. Forgotten Books uses state-of-the-art technology to digitally reconstruct the work, preserving the original format whilst repairing imperfections present in the aged copy. In rare cases, an imperfection in the original, such as a blemish or missing page, may be replicated in our edition. We do, however, repair the vast majority of imperfections successfully; any imperfections that remain are intentionally left to preserve the state of such historical works.

Forgotten Books is a registered trademark of FB &c Ltd.
Copyright © 2018 FB &c Ltd.
FB &c Ltd, Dalton House, 60 Windsor Avenue, London, SW19 2RR.
Company number 08720141. Registered in England and Wales.

For support please visit www.forgottenbooks.com

LIBRARY OF CONGRESS.

Chap. _____ Copyright No. _____
           Shelf JK 246
                  W 5

UNITED STATES OF AMERICA.

A Proposed New Constitution

—FOR THE—

UNITED STATES.

By JAMES C. WEST.

FIRST EDITION.

Published By James C. West,
Nixa, Missouri.

A Proposed

New Constitution

—FOR THE—

UNITED STATES.

By JAMES C. WEST.

FIRST EDITION

PUBLISHED BY JAMES C. WEST,
Nixa, Missouri.

Copyrighted 1890, by James C. West.

INVOCATION.

> "Long live the man in early contest found,
> Who spoke his heart when dastards trembled round,
> Who fired with more than Greek or Roman rage,
> Flashed truth on tyrants from his manly page—"

Hail, ye who are yet patriotic freemen! Ye who love LIBERTY, want LIBERTY, and will die for LIBERTY! Ye who have, and will lay aside prejudice, and heed the precepts of the Goddess of Liberty! Ye who are bound in the shackles of "wage slavery!" Ye who are ensconced behind your millions! Ye from the highest to the lowest, whether in palace or hovel, all hail!! You I invoke; to you I address my views of humane government. Musing upon the conditions now existing, with that insatiate love of true born liberty, equity, and fraternity, I view a scene which I fain would dispel; a scene which is not fancy, nor theatrical, nor viewed in dreamy slumbers, but a dreadful reality, to the sorrow of my fellow-beings. Of you I ask a favor, that will benefit not only a few, but the worthy whole: that you will act with the prudence that our fore-fathers of 1776 displayed, when they divorced themselves from the tyrannical government of King George III; that you will timely, and judiciously use the propriety of the ballot——

To you I dedicate the good of this little volume, that you may read and comprehend is my wish.

JAMES C. WEST.

GRATITUDE.

To the kindness of J. C. Cravens, lawyer, of Springfield, Mo., I feel greatly indebted for the use of his Statutes of the United States, which demonstrated to me the existence of national conspiracy; also, from which I copied some of the iniquitous laws to which I have referred to in this little volume. Nor am I less indebted to my friend Jacob Hartley, for the use of a book containing the President's messages, from which I gleaned the spirit of the framers of our Constitution; but now I find said spirit banished from the halls of Congress.

PREFACE.

"The pen is mightier than the sword."

This being a new subject, a new idea to the civilized world; and not knowing how it will be accepted by my people; it is with some degree of timidity and awkardness that I enter on this plan of relief.

The design of this little volume is, not to make its content obligatory upon the people of the United States, but to call a halt in that course which so many nations have followed to their downfall, and are recorded on the pages of history among the pale nations of the dead, as a failure in humane government.

My purpose being to investigate the basic rules of government, which should be included in all constitutions, whether in America, Europe, Asia or Africa. Also to call attention to the fact that all constitutions are interpreted by men, that have the "authority;" and that men get said "authority" through the "power" of the ballot or the bullet; and, that said "power," which gives "authority" to men, to interpret Constitutions, and make the law of nations, which govern the rich and poor, the high and low, has been THE MONEY POWER; this fact is verified by the history of all nations subject to the sways of human nature. And now I call your attention to the necessity of making all Constitutions an interpretation of their own provisions; and making their provisions especially for the benefit of laboring classes who earn by the sweat of the brow; and let aristocracy take care of themselves; but take care that the aristocracy is bridled, and that the reins are in the hands of the tillers of the soil; and that the tillers of the soil are owners in fee-simple; and that they have a constitutional power to guard their own liberty, and the liberty of all posterity.

Therefore I present herein a Constitution for the people of the United States, and do not think that it contains all that I want in the Constitution which governs me; but I only wish to show the principle which should be acted upon without delay.

I am aware that I will be charged with sacrilege, and that there will be severe criticism by both reformers and conservatives; but that will not injure my cause, for it will be the cause of an investigation, and the truth will be revealed, justice will be defended, and my people shall not die martyrs to the cause of LIBERTY—if I do.

I pardon all condemnation; I ask not for revenge; but will contend for the "rights" of my fellow-beings; the moral rights, the just rights, to which I have a right by the virtue of my existence in this world; and not the right to live, provided I serve the "money lords" of creation.

THE AUTHOR.

"Thy spirit Independence, O let me share,
Lord of lion heart and eagle eye,
They steps I'll follow with my bosom bare,
Nor heed the storm that howls along the sky!"

DECLARATION OF INDEPENDENCE,

ADOPTED BY CONGRESS JULY 4, 1776.

A DECLARATION BY THE REPRESENTATIVES OF THE UNITED STATES OF AMERICA, IN CONGRESS ASSEMBLED.

When, in the course of human events, it becomes necessary for one people to dissolve the political bands which have connected them with another, and to assume among the powers of the earth the separate and equal station to which the laws of nature and of nature's God entitle them, a decent respect to the opinions of mankind requires that they should declare the causes which impel them to the separation.

We hold these truths to be self-evident, that all men are created equal, that they are endowed by their Creator with certain unalienable rights; that among these are life, liberty, and the pursuit of happiness: that, to secure these rights, governments are instituted among men, deriving their just powers from the consent of the governed; that, whenever any form of government becomes destructive of these ends, it is the right of the people to alter or abolish it, and institute a new government, laying its foundation on such principles, and organizing its powers in such form, as to them shall seem most likely to effect their safety and happiness. Prudence, indeed, will dictate that governments should not be changed for light and transient causes; and, accordingly, all experience hath shown that mankind are more disposed to suffer, while evils are sufferable, than to right themselves by abolishing the forms to which they are accustomed. But when a long train of abuses and usurpations, pursuing invariation the same object, evinces a design to reduce them under absolute despotism, it is their right, it is their duty, to throw off such government, and to provide new guards for their future security.

—8—

Such has been the patient sufferance of the people of the United States, and such is now the necessity which constrains them to alter former systems of government. The history of the government of the United States, for the past thirty years is: a history of repeated injuries and usurpations, all having in direct object the establishment of absolute tyranny over the states of the United States.

To prove this, let facts be submitted to a candid world:—

That past and present rulers of the United States for the last thirty years has enacted a code of laws especially for the benefit of a "favored few" to the exclusion of the toiling many; that among this code, the following acts are a few of the most prominent:—

1. The establishment of an excessive high protective tariff system.
2. The "exception clause" on the Treasury notes, issued Feb. 25, 1862.
3. The issueing of interest bearing bonds for every dollar of money issued during our last Civil War.
4. The establishment of a National Banking System.
5. The contraction of the currency in 1866.
6. The act pledging the payment of the United States Bonds in coin.
7. The repeal of the Income Tax Law.
8. The demonitization of silver, and thereby making gold the only standard of value.

9. The granting of the publc domain to corporations ot local nature.

10. The allowance of "money kings" to combine and exact exorbitant prices on the articles consumed by the tillers of the soil; and to pool and combine, thereby killing all free competition and honest industries; and that the following is the result of said and similar legislation:—

That they have encouraged and excited that insatiate love of money, love of wealth, love of power to rule and live in luxury off that which they extort from honest labor; until the "vampire money power" can afford to spend millions of money in buying traitorous, eloquent orators, and subsidizing the press, and issuing campaign circulars to blind and prejudice the people, so that it can "legally and illegally" steal hundreds of millions from an innocent, slavish and toiling people through "unjust legislation;" that millions of money are hoarded in the Treasury of the United States, while millions of people are suffering from want of sufficient circulating medium; that a majority of farmers, who produce the bread of life, have been, and are being compelled to mortgage their homes in order to live, and carry on their business under existing conditions; that the land and wealth of this nation are rapidly centralizing into the hands of a few men, evincing a tendency to subvert the rights granted to us by our forefathers of 1776; that general discontent has been created, halls of peace are converted into halls of sedition, and our country is honeycombed with secret organizations.

THE CONSTITUTION.

NOTE.—A figure is placed at the beginning of each paragraph of the following copy of the Constitution, so that the paragraphs may be referred to by numbers.

1. We, the people of the United States, in order to form a more perfect union, establish justice, insure domestic tranquillity, provide for the common defense, promote the general welfare, and secure the blessings of liberty to ourselves and our posterity, do ordain and establish this Constitution for the United States of America.

ARTICLE I.

SECTION I.

2. All legislative powers herein granted shall be vested in a Congress of the United States, which shall consist of a Senate and House of Representatives.

SECTION 2.

3. The House of Representatives shall be composed of members chosen every second year by the people of the several States, and the electors in each State shall have the qualifications requisite for electors of the most numerous branch of the State Legislature.

4. No person shall be a representative who shall not have attained to the age of twenty-five years; also, he shall be a natural born American citizen, and be an inhabitant of the state in which he shall be chosen.

5. Representatives shall be apportioned among the several states which may be included within this Union according to their respective numbers, which shall be determined by the last census, including all persons, except Indians, not taxed.

6. The number of representatives shall be one for every 175,000 persons, counting the whole number of persons, except Indians not taxed; also, one for every fraction over, provided, said fraction exceed 100,000 persons.

7. No person can become a member of the House of Representatives who is worth over $25,000, or has any claim to any property worth over $25,000.

8. When vacancies happen in the representation from any State, the executive authority thereof shall issue writs of election to fill such vacancies.

9. The House of Representatives shall choose their Speaker and other officers, and shall have the sole power of impeaching its members and officers, and no person shall be convicted without concurrence of two-thirds of the members present.

SECTION 3.

10. The Senate of the United States shall be composed of two Senators from each State, chosen each presidential election, by the qualified voters thereof for four years; and each Senator shall have one vote.

11. No person shall be a Senator who shall not have attained to the age of thirty-five years; also, he shall be a natural born American citizen, and be an inhabitant of the State for which he is chosen.

12. No person can become a member of the Senate who is worth over $50,000, or has at his command or any claim to property worth over $50,000.

13. The Vice-President of the United States shall be President of the Senate, but shall have no vote unless they be equally divided.

14. The Senate shall choose their other officers, and also a President *pro tempore* in the absence of the Vice-President, or when he shall exercise the office of President of the United States.

15. The Senate shall have the sole power to impeach its own members and officers. When sitting for that purpose, they shall be on oath or affirmation. When the President of the United States is tried, the Chief Justice shall preside; and no person shall be convicted without the concurrence of two-thirds of the members present.

SECTION 4.

16. The times, places, and manner of holding elections for Senators and Representatives shall be prescribed in each State by the Legislature thereof; but the Congress may at any time, by law, make or alter such regulations.

17. The Congress shall assemble at least once in every year; and such meeting shall be on

the second Monday in January, unless they shall by law appoint a different day.

SECTION 5.

18. Each House shall be the judge of the election returns, and qualifications of its own members; and a three-fourths majority of its members shall constitute a quorum to do business, but a smaller number shall adjourn from day to day; and in case the absent members are physically unable to attend, a three-fourths majority of the healthy members shall constitute a quorum; but in case the absent members of good health refuse or fail to be present in the assembly, without a reasonable excuse, a majority of the members present shall proceed to impeach said members.

19. When vacancies happen in either House, the presiding officer thereof shall inform the executive authority of the unrepresented State or States; and it shall be the duty of such authority, within ten days after such information is received, to issue writs of election to fill such vacancies.

20. Each House shall determine the rules for its proceedings, censure its members for any action, expell any of its members for not complying with the provisions of this Constitution, or for disorderly behavior, and with the concurrent vote of two-thirds of its members, it shall impeach any person violating any provision of this Constitution, and forever debar said member from holding any office of public trust under the

United States, unless such disability be removed by the concurrent vote of three-fourths of the members of the House from which he was expelled.

21. Each House shall keep a journal of its proceedings, and from time to time publish the same, excepting such parts as may in their estimation require secrecy; and the yeas and nays of either House on any bill, question, order or resolution shall be entered on the journal.

SECTION 5.

22. No person can become a member of either House who has not labored five years, after he has attained to the age of ten years, at either agricultural or some mechanical art.

23. All members of each House shall be subject to the call of the President; and shall be required to assemble once every year; and the Senate shall assemble once every year; and the Senate shall assemble at any time the House of Representatives shall assemble; and members of each House shall vote *viva voce* for or against all bills, motions, orders or resolutions that shall come before them.

24. All members of each House shall be required to take the following oath: "I, ———, do solemnly swear, (or affirm), that I will do everything within my power to carry out the provisions of this Constitution, and do the greatest good to the greatest number; that I will not approve of anything contrary to the spirit of this Constitu-

tion, either expressed or implied; that if I willfully violate one precept or letter, I ask the vengeance of God upon me, and the universal detestation of mankind."

25. Judgment in cases of impeachment shall not extend further than to removal from office, and disqualification to hold and enjoy any office of honor, trust, or profit, under the United States; but the party convicted shall nevertheless be liable and subject to indictment, trial, judgment, and punishment, according to law.

26. All members of each House shall be required to attend all through each session, each day and each hour; and no member shall be excused, unless in case of dangerous sickness of himself or family; and no member shall be allowed to pair votes with any other member or members.

27. Neither House, during the session of Congress, shall, without the consent of the other, adjourn for more than three days, nor to any other place than that in which the two Houses shall be sitting.

SECTION 6.

28. The Senators and Representatives shall receive a compensation for their services, to be ascertained by law, and paid out of the treasury of the United States. They shall in all cases, except treason, felony, and breach of the peace, be privileged from arrest during their attendance at the session of their respective Houses, and in go-

ing to and returning from the same; and for any speech or debate in either House, they shall not be questioned in any other place.

29. No Senator or Representative shall receive a compensation exceeding fifteen times the average amount of wages paid to laboring farm hands per year, counting 365 days per year minus 52 Sundays, said average to be ascertained for the report of the Commissioner of Agriculture; except the Speaker of the House and President of the Senate, who shall receive twenty-five times said average amount and no more; except an allowance for stationery, newspapers and mileage, which shall be determined by Congress, but shall be no more than is actually and needfully required; but in case of war prices they shall receive according to the wages existing prior to said event.

30. No Senator or Representative shall, during the time for which he was elected, be appointed to any civil office under the authority of the United States which has been created, or the emoluments whereof have been increased, during such time; and no person holding any office under the United States shall be a member of either House during his continuance in office.

SECTION 7.

31. Every bill shall originate and be passed or defeated as follows: "It shall be titled according to the object of its contents; and shall be signed by at least ten members, and presented to

to the proper officer, then shall be referred to the committee having jurisdiction over it; said committee shall translate it into proper legal form, but shall not change it so as to defeat the object of the originator; if he has any objections to the form he shall state them, and the bill shall be changed till satisfactory with the originator, then it shall be read and presented to the House for discussion and vote, and every member shall vote *viva voce* for or against said bill, and the yeas and nays and names of persons voting shall be recorded in the journal; if said bill is passed by a majority vote of both Houses, it shall then be presented to the President of the United States; if he approve, he shall sign it, then it shall become law according to its provisions; if he disapprove, he shall return it, with his objections, to that House in which it originated, who shall enter the objections on their journal, and proceed to reconsider it; if after such reconsideration, two-thirds of that House shall agree to pass the bill, it shall be sent, together with the objections, to the other House, by which it shall be likewise considered; and if approved by two-thirds of that House, it shall become a law. If any bill shall not be returned by the President within ten days (Sundays excepted) after it shall have been presented to him, the same shall become a law in like manner, as if he had signed it, unless the Congress by their adjournment prevent its return; in which case it shall not become a law.

32. All bills for raising or reducing the revenue shall originate in the House of Representatives; but the Senate may propose or concur with amendments.

33. All bills relating to the Finances of the United States, or Constitutional amendments, shall originate in the House of Representatives, and shall not be vetoed by either the President or Senate, if it passed the House of Representatives by a concurrent vote of two-thirds of its members; but such bills shall be presented to the President, and if he sign it, it shall become a law according to its provisions; but if he refuse to sign it, he shall send the bill, with his objections to the House of Representatives, within ten days after he received such bill; then they shall proceed to reconsider, and if passed again by a concurrent vote of two-thirds of its members, it shall become a law to be executed.

34. Every order, resolution, or bill passed by both Houses, or all Finance bills and bills of Constitutional Amendment, which passed the House of Representatives by a concurrent vote of two-thirds of its members, shall be presented to the President of the United States, and before the same shall go into effect, it shall be approved by him, or, if disapproved he shall send it back, with his objections, to the House in which it originated and be treated according to the rules and limitations prescribed in case of a bill.

SECTION 8.

The Congress shall have power,—

35. To lay and collect taxes, duties, imposts, and excises, to pay the debts, and provide for the common defense and general welfare, of the United States; but all duties, imposts, and excises shall be uniform throughout the United States;

36. But, shall not lay nor collect taxes, duties, imposts, and excises to such an excess, that money will accumulate in the treasury, more than is requisite for the necessary expenses of the Government of the United States;

37. And shall have power to, and shall lay a tax on the sumptuousness of the people of the United States; also, shall levy a graduated income and land tax; and all notes, mortgages and bonds, against the Government of the United States, or any individual, held or owned by any person, shall be taxable for one half the face value; and all such notes, mortgages, or bonds of any sort, shall be entered on the tax books, or become non-collectable by any court in law;

39. To borrow money on the credit of the United States;

40. Congress shall have no right to borrow on the credit of the United States, except in case of war or insurrection; and then not until the circulating medium has been increased to $60 sixty dollars per capita; and shall not issue any bonds of any kind until the per capita circulation surpasses sixty dollars;

41. To regulate commerce with foreign nations, and among the several States, and with the Indian tribes;

42. Congress shall make it a crime for any individual or corporation to attempt to, or make an arbitrary price, on any product consumed, or produced in the United States; also, any person or corporation who shall wilfully and knowingly engage in any pool, combine, trust or rebate system, shall be punished by imprisonment not less then three years; also, shall not make any appropriation of public property to corporations of a local nature;

43. To establish a uniform rule of naturalization, and uniform laws on the subject of bankruptcies, and shall make all interest laws uniform throughout the United States;

44. To coin or issue money, regulate the value thereof, and of foreign coin, and fix the standard of weights and measures;

45. And shall have power to, and shall swell the circulating medium of the people of the United States to forty dollars per capita, and maintain it at that throughout the perpituity of this Constitution; said per capita to be determined by the Superintendent of the Census, every year, and accepted by Congress, who shall order the Treasurer to issue the estimated amount, which shall be subject to the expenditures and demands of the Government of the United States;

46. Congress shall make all moneys a legal

tender for all debts, with no exception; and shall issue no interest or non-interest bearing bonds to maintain a forty dollar per capita circulating medium.

47. Congress shall not delegate to any individual or corporation the power to regulate or issue a single dollar of the volume of money, except the Treasurer by order of Congress;

48. Congress shall make it a crime of treason for any person to attempt to depreciate any money of the United States; or receive, or buy, any dollar for less or more than one hundred cents; or to counterfeit any of the United States notes or securities;

49. To provide for the punishment of counterfeiting the securies, treasury notes and current coin of the United States;

50. To establish post-offices and post-roads;

51. To promote the progress of science and useful arts, by securing for limited times, to authors and inventors, the exclusive right to their respective writings and discoveries;

52. To constitute tribunals inferior to the Supreme Court;

53. To define and punish piracies and felonies committed on the high seas, and offenses against the law of nations;

54. To declare war, grant letters of marque and reprisal, and make rules concerning captures on land and water;

55. To raise and support armies;

56. But all moneys appropriated in raising and supporting armies shall be gradually withdrawn from circulation by taxation, and destroyed, and no bonds issued in their place, within ten years after the war; provided, the amount does not exceed sixty dollars per capita; and in case the amount exceed sixty dollars per capita time shall be extended one year for every one hundred millions of dollars issued over said amount; and all bonds issued for the support of armies by order of Congress, shall be redeemed in any legal currency of the United States, after the circulation has been reduced to forty dollars per capita at the rate of one hundred millions of dollars per year; and any person holding bonds against the United States, shall deliver the same to the Treasurer of the United States, upon demand, within thirty days (Sundays excepted) after receiving such notice; and any person refusing to deliver, or demanding a premium for such bonds, shall forfeit his right to such bonds, and they shall be confiscated to the Government of the United States.

57. To provide and maintain a navy;

58. To provide and maintain a navy; but in case of invasion, war or insurrection, all appropriations for increase of navy and maintenance of such increase shall be subject to the same rules and limitations of supporting armies.

59. To make rules for the government and regulation of the land and naval forces;

60. To provide for calling forth the militia to

execute the laws of the Union, suppress insurrections, and repel invasions;

61. To provide for organizing, arming, and disciplining the militia, and for governing such part of them as may be employed in the service of the United States, reserving to the State respectively the appointment of the officers, and the authority of training the militia according to the discipline prescribed by Congress;

62. To compensate every officer created under this Constitution; but shall compensate according to their own salary, considering the amount of actual labor performed, and the amount of accomplishments requisite to perform said labor, and with a view of justice and economy;

63. To exercise exclusive legislation in all cases whatsoever over such district (not exceeding ten miles square) as may, by cession of particular States and the acceptance of Congress, become the seat of the Government of the United States; and to exercise like authority over all places purchased, by the consent of the Legislature of the State in which the same shall be, for the erection of forts, magazines, arsenals, dockyards, and other needful buildings. And,—

64. To make all laws which shall be necessary and proper for carrying into execution the foregoing powers, and all other powers vested in this Constitution in the Government of the United States, or in any department or officer thereof.

SECTION 9.

65. The immigration or importation of such persons as Congress thinks are detrimental, and not promoting the general welfare, shall be prohibited by statutory laws.

66. The privilege of the writ of *habeas corpus* shall not be suspended, unless when, in cases of rebellion or invasion, the public safety may require it.

67. No bill of attainer, or *ex-post-facto* law, shall be passed.

68. No capitation tax shall be laid, unless in proportion to the census or enumeration hereinbefore directed to be taken.

69. No tax or duty shall be laid on articles exported from any State. No preference shall be given by any regulation of commerce or revenue to the ports of one State over those of another; nor shall vessels bound to or from one State be obliged to enter, clear, or pay duties in another.

70. No money shall be drawn from the treasury but in consequence of appropriations made by law; and a regular statement and account of the receipts and expenditures of all money shall be published from time to time.

71. No title of nobility shall be granted by the United States; and no person holding any office of profit or trust under them shall, without the consent of the Congress, accept of any present, emolument, office, or title, of any kind whatever, from any king, prince, or foreign state.

SECTION 10.

72. No State shall enter into any treaty, alliance, or confederation; grant letters of marque and reprisal; coin money; emit bills and credits; make any thing but the legal money of the United States a tender in payment for debts; pass any bill of attainder, *ex-post-facto* law, or law impairing the obligation of contracts; or grant any title of nobility.

73. No State shall, without the consent of the Congress, lay any imposts or duties on imporrts or exports, except what may be absolutely necessary for executing its inspection laws; and the net produce of all duties and imposts laid by any State on imports or exports shall be for the use of the treasury of the United States, and all such laws shall be subject to the revision and control of the Congress. No State shall without the consent of Congress, lay any duty of tonnage, keep troops or ships-of-war in time of peace, enter into any agreement or compact with another State or with a foreign power, or engage in war, unless actually invaded, or in such imminent danger as will not admit of delay.

ARTICLE II.

SECTION 1.

74. The executive power shall be vested in a President of the United States of America. He shall hold his office during the term of four years,

and together with the Vice-President chosen for the same term, be elected as follows:—

75. He shall be elected by the qualified voters of the United States, having the qualifictions requisite to the electors of the most numerous branch of the State Legislature; and the candidate for President, also the candidate for Vice-President receiving the largest number of votes, shall act as President and Vice-President of the United States.

76. No person except a natural born citizen of the United States, shall be eligible to the office of President; neither shall any person be elligible to such office who shall not have attained to the age of thirty-five years, and have been fourteen years a resident within the United States; or, who shall have served one term as President of the United States; and no person constitutionally inelligible to the office of President, shall be elligible to the office of Vice-President.

77. The President shall at stated times by order of Congress, receive for his services a compensation, which shall not exceed one hundred and twenty-five times the average amount of wages paid to laboring farm hands per year, counting 365 days one year; said average to be determined from report of Commissioner of Agriculture; but in case of war prices, he shall receive according to the prices prior to said event; and he shall not receive, within his term of office, any other emolument from the United States, or any

of them; except an allowance to be made by Congress, for stationery, household expense, mileage to and from the Capitol to his home once a year, but no allowance shall be Constitutional, that exceed actual needs, and within the purview of economy and justice.

78. Before he shall enter on the execution of his office, he shall take the following oath or affirmation:— I —— —— do solemnly swear or affirm that I will faithfully execute the office of President of the United States; and will to the best of my ability preserve, protect, and defend the Constitution of the United States; and that I will not approve of any thing contrary to the spirit of our Constitution, or disapprove of any thing in accordance with the Constitution of the United States, either by actions expressed or implied; and, that if I wilfully violate one precept or letter, I ask the vengeance of God upon me, and the universal detestation or mankind.

79. In case of the removal of the President from office, or of his death, resignation, or inability to discharge the powers and duties of the said office, the same shall devolve on the Vice-President; and the Congress may by law provide for the case of removal, death, resignation, or inability, both of the President and Vice-President, declaring what officer shall then act as President, and such officer shall act accordingly until the disability be removed, or a President shall be elected.

and together with the Vice-President chosen for the same term, be elected as follows:—

75. He shall be elected by the qualified voters of the United States, having the qualifictions requisite to the electors of the most numerous branch of the State Legislature; and the candidate for President, also the candidate for Vice-President receiving the largest number of votes, shall act as President and Vice-President of the United States.

76. No person except a natural born citizen of the United States, shall be eligible to the office of President; neither shall any person be elligible to such office who shall not have attained to the age of thirty-five years, and have been fourteen years a resident within the United States; or, who shall have served one term as President of the United States; and no person constitutionally inelligible to the office of President, shall be elligible to the office of Vice-President.

77. The President shall at stated times by order of Congress, receive for his services a compensation, which shall not exceed one hundred and twenty-five times the average amount of wages paid to laboring farm hands per year, counting 365 days one year; said average to be determined from report of Commissioner of Agriculture; but in case of war prices, he shall receive according to the prices prior to said event; and he shall not receive, within his term of office, any other emolument from the United States, or any

of them; except an allowance to be made by Congress, for stationery, household expense, mileage to and from the Capitol to his home once a year, but no allowance shall be Constitutional, that exceed actual needs, and within the purview of economy and justice.

78. Before he shall enter on the execution of his office, he shall take the following oath or affirmation:— I —— —— do solemnly swear or affirm that I will faithfully execute the office of President of the United States; and will to the best of my ability preserve, protect, and defend the Constitution of the United States; and that I will not approve of any thing contrary to the spirit of our Constitution, or disapprove of any thing in accordance with the Constitution of the United States, either by actions expressed or implied; and, that if I wilfully violate one precept or letter, I ask the vengeance of God upon me, and the universal detestation or mankind.

79. In case of the removal of the President from office, or of his death, resignation, or inability to discharge the powers and duties of the said office, the same shall devolve on the Vice-President; and the Congress may by law provide for the case of removal, death, resignation, or inability, both of the President and Vice-President, declaring what officer shall then act as President, and such officer shall act accordingly until the disability be removed, or a President shall be elected.

SECTION 2.

80. The President shall be commander-in-chief of the army and navy of the United States, and of the militia of the several States when called into the actual service of the United States: he may require the opinion, in writing, of the principal officer in each of the executive departments, upon any subject relating to the duties of their respective offices; and he shall have power to grant repreives and pardons for offenses against the United States, except in cases of impeachment.

81. He shall have power, by and with the advice and consent of the Senate, to make treaties, provided two-thirds of the Senators present concur; and he shall nominate, and by and with the advice and consent of the Senate shall appoint, ambassadors, other public ministers, and consuls, judges of the Supreme Court, and all other officers of the United States whose appointments are not herein otherwise provided for, and which shall be established by law: but the Congress may by law vest the appointment of such inferior officers as they think proper in the President alone, in the courts of law, or in the heads of departments.

SECTION 3.

82. He shall, from time to time, give to the Congress information of the state of the Union, and recommend to their consideration such measures as he shall judge necessary and expedient; he may, on extraordinary occasions, convene both

Houses or either of them; he shall receive ambassadors and other public ministers; he shall take care that the laws be faithfully executed, and shall commission all the officers of the United States.

83. And in case of a disagreement between the two Houses, with respect to adjournment of session, a majority vote of the House of Representatives shall determine the time.

SECTION 4.

84. The President, Vice-President, and all civil officers of the United States, shall be removed from office on impeachment for, and conviction of, treason, bribery, or other high crimes and misdemeanors.

ARTICLE III.

SECTION 1.

85. The judicial power of the United States shall be vested in one Supreme Court, and in such inferior courts as Congress may, from time to time, ordain and establish.

86. The judges, both of the supreme and inferior courts, shall hold their offices during good behavior; and shall, at stated times, receive for their services a compensation, which shall not be dimished during their continuance in office.

SECTION 2.

1. The judicial power shall extend to all cases in law and equity arising under this Con-

stitution, the laws of the United States, and treatist made or which shall be made under their authority; to all cases affecting ambassadors, other public ministers, and consuls; to all cases of admirality and maritine jurisdiction; to controversies to which the United States shall be a party; (to controversies between two or more States,) between a State and citizens of another State between citizens of different States, between citizens of the same State claiming lands under grants of different States, and between a State, or the citizens thereof, and foreign states, citizens, or subjects.

88. In all cases affecting ambassadors, other public ministers, and consuls, and those in which a State shall be a party, the Supreme Court shall have original jurisdiction. In all the other cases before mentioned, the Supreme Court shall have appellate jurisdiction, both as to law and fact, with such exceptions and under such regulations as the Congress shall make.

89. The trial of all crimes, except in cases of impeachment, shall be by jury; and such trial shall be held in the State where the said crimes shall have been committed: but when not committed within any State, the trial shall be at such place or places as the Congress may by law have directed, but the Supreme Court shall not have power to abrogate any law affecting the finances of the United States, which passed the House of Representatives, or can be passed said

House by a concurrant vote of two-thirds of its members.

90. Treason against the United States shall consist only in levying war against them, or in adhering to their enemies, giving them aid and comfort. No person shall be convicted of treason, unless on the testimony of two witnesses to the same overt act, or on confession in open court.

91. The Congress shall have power to declare the punishment of treason; but no attainder of treason shall work corruption of blood, or forfeiture, except during the life of the person attained.

ARTICLE IV.

SECTION 1.

92. Full faith and credit shall be given in each State to the public acts, records, and judicial proceedings, of every other State. And the Congress may, by general laws, prescribe the manner in which such acts, records, and proceedings shall be proved, and the effect thereof.

SECTION 2.

93. The citizens of each State shall be entitled to all privileges and immunities of citizens in the several States.

94. A person charged in any State with treason, felony, or other crime, who shall flee from justice and be found in another State, shall, on demand of the executive authority of the State

from which he fled, be delivered up, to be removed to the State having jurisdiction of the crime.

95. No person held to service or labor in one State under the laws thereof, escaping into another, shall, in consequence of any law or regulation therein, be discharged from such service or labor, but shall be delivered up on claim of the party to whom such service or labor may be due.

SECTION 3.

96. New States may be admitted by the Congress into this Union; but no new State shall be formed or erected within the jurisdiction of any other State, nor any State be formed by th ejunction of two or more States, or parts of States, without the consent of the legislatures of the States concerned, as well as of the Congress.

97. The Congress shall have power to dispose of and make all needful rules and regulations respecting the territory, or other property, belonging to the United States; and nothing in this Constitution shall be so construed as to prejudice any claims of the United States or of any particular State.

SECTION 4.

98. The United States shall guarantee to every State in this Union a republican form of government, and shall protect each of them against invasion, and, on application of the legislature or of the executive (when the legislature can not be convened), against domestic violence.

ARTICLE V.

99. The Congress, whenever two-thirds of both Houses shall deem it necessary, shall propose amendment to this constitution, or, on the application of the legislatures of two-thirds of the several States, shall call a convention for proposing amendments, which, in either case, shall be valid to all intents and purposes as part of this Constitution, when ratified by the legislatures of three-fourths of the several States, or by conventions in three-fourths thereof, as the one or the other mode of ratification may be proposed by the Congress: provided that no amendment shall be made, which will render null and void any provision of this Constitution, unless such amendment be made by the concurrence of three-fourths of the members of a full House; and then be presented to the people to be voted upon by yeas and nays at tha next general election, and a majority vote shall adopt or reject; and to make an additional amendment, only a concurrent vote of three-fourths of the members of the House of Representatives, shall be necessary.

ARTICLE VI.

100. All debts contracted, and engagements entered into, before the adoption of this Constitution, shall be as valid against the United States, under this Constitution, as under the old Constitution.

101. The phrase "as valid" shall not be construed to mean that all obligations shall be fulfilled, unless said obligations are in harmony with this Constitution or justice between man and man, or Government and subject.

102. The Senators and Representatives before mentioned, and the members of the several State legislatures, and all executive and judicial officers both of the United States and the several States, shall be bound by oath or affirmation to support this Constitution; but no religious test shall ever be required as a qualification to any office or public trust under the United States.

ARTICLE VII.

103. The ratifications of the Conventions of two-thirds of the States shall be sufficient for the establishment of this Constitution between the States so ratifying the same.

MISCELLANEOUS PROVISIONS.

ARTICLE I.

104. Congress shall make no law respecting an establishment of religion, or probibiting the free exercise thereof; or abridging the freedom of speech or of the press; or the right of the people peaceably to assemble, and to petition the government for a redress of grievances.

ARTICLE II.

105. A well-regulated militia being necessary to the security of a free State, the right of the people to keep and bear arms shall not be infringed.

ARTICLE III.

106. No soldier shall, in time of peace, be quartered in any house without the consent of the owner; nor in time of war but in a manner prescribed by law.

ARTICLE IV.

107. The right of the people to be secure in their persons, houses, papers and effects, against unreasonable searches and seizures, shall not be violated; and no warrants shall issue but upon probable cause, supported by oath or affirmation, and particularly describing the place to be searched, and the persons or things to be seized.

ARTICLE V.

108. No person shall be held to answer for a capital or otherwise infamous crime, unless on a presentment or indictment of a grand jury, except in cases arising in the land or naval forces, or in the militia, when in actual service, in time of war or public danger; nor shall any person be subject, for the same offense, to be twice put in jeopardy of life or limb; nor shall be compelled in any criminal case, to be a witness against him-

self; nor be deprived of life, liberty or property without due process of law; nor shall private property be taken for public use, without just compensation.

ARTICLE VI.

109. In all criminal prosecutions, the accused shall enjoy the right to a speedy and public trial by an impartial jury of the State and district wherein the crime shall have been committed, which district shall have been previously ascertained by law; and to be informed of the nature and cause of the accusation; to be confronted with the witnesses against him; to have compulsory process for obtaining witnesses in his favor; and to have the assistance of counsel for his defense.

ARTICLE VII.

110. In suits at common law, where the value in controversy shall exceed twenty dollars, the right of trial by jury shall be preserved; and no fact, tried by a jury, shall be otherwise re-examined in any court of the United States than according to the rules of the common law.

ARTICLE VIII.

111. Excessive bail shall not be required, nor excessive fines imposed, nor cruel and unusual punishments inflicted.

ARTICLE IX.

112. The enumeration in the Constitution of certain rights shall not be construed to deny or disparage others retained by the people.

ARTICLE X.

113. The powers not delegated to the United States by the Constitution, nor prohibited by it to the States, are reserved to the States respectively, or to the people.

ARTICLE XI.

114. The judicial power of the United States shall not be construed to extend to any suit in law or equity commenced or prosecuted against one of the United States by citizens of another State, or by citizens or subjects of any foreign State.

ARTICLE XIII.

116. Neither slavery nor involuntary servitude, except as a punishment for crime, whereof the party shall have been duly convicted, shall exist within the United States, or any place subject to their jurisdiction.

ARTICLE XIV.

117. All persons born or naturalized in the United States, and subject to the jurisdiction thereof, are citizens of the United States and of

the State wherein they reside. No State shall make or enforce any law which shall abridge the privileges or immunities of citizens of the United States; nor shall any State deprive any person of life, liberty, or property, without due process of law, nor deny to any person within its jurisdiction the equal protection of the laws.

117. But neither the United States nor any State shall assume or pay any debt or obligation incurred in aid of insurrection or rebellion against the United States, or any claim for the loss or emancipation of any slave; but all such debts, obligations, and claims, shall be held illegal and void.

ARTICLE XV.

118. The right of the citizens of the United States to vote shall not be denied or abridged by the United States or any State on account of race, color, or previous condition of servitude.

THE VINDICATION OF THIS PROPOSED NEW CONSTITUTION.

NOTE.— I shall refer you to each paragraph by number. Then, I request you to turn and read the paragraph which has the number on the left of its margin.

No. 1. I now refer you to the Preamble, No. 1. I leave this unchanged, for it covers all the ground necessary; it demands enough to secure peace, prosperity, and perpetual liberty to any people.

No. 4. This forbids any man to become a member, unless he is a natural born American citizen. The reason why is: to prevent a foreigner from representing the people of the United States. I deny their being capable of representing true Americanism; but don't understand, that I mean that they are all unpatriotic; for some foreigners are more ardent lovers of America, than of their mother country. But in case of foreign war, the foreigner would be likely to show a preference between their mother country and other countries. As it is the nature of man, to have a prejudice against a country that has in time past, done his mother country an injury. The history of the World, is a history of war, almost without cessation. Therefore, there is surely some prejudice in the mind of any foreigner; hence they must not be allowed the privilege of representing the people of the United States of America.

No. 6. This clause is to prevent the House from being composed of an insufficient number to insure representation. And with the view that one man can represent this number of persons justly, and no more, that is, not many more.

No. 7. This clause is to put a break on the money power, that is, to some extent; so that the Government will not drift into an aristocratic Government; and for the reason that an exceeding rich man will not legislate for the interest of a laboring man.

No. 10. This clause is changed, and the mode of electing Senators is given to the direct vote of the people: for the reason that it is the best to obtain the voice of the people; that it is easier to buy a majority vote of the legislature, than to buy a majority of the popular vote. And the time of electing is changed to the election of the President, for the reason that a Senate and a President elected at the same time would be more likely to agree, on account of their being elected on the same issues. And the Senate would go out of power in case the people changed their politics, and enthroned a different political power; hence there would be more harmony between the people, legislative and executive powers. There are many reasons for this clause, and I can't take the space to enumerate all. In the eyes of justice it carries conviction, without any further argument.

No. 11. This change is for the same reason as regards Representatives. See No. 4.

No. 12. This is to rout the millionaires out of the hall of legislatures, for similar reasons used in defense of No. 7.

No. 17. This change in assembling is made for the reason that when Congress assembles in December it has to adjourn during holidays; and according to this change they will commence after holidays, and they need not be to the expense of coming home to spend the holidays, but proceed with their business without interruption until their adjournment.

No. 18. The object of this clause is to have all members of Congress present during the enactment of laws; and then all the people will be represented. The history of the past shows that a bare majority has been doing the legislation, while the balance were on a pleasure trip, or fishing tour, that were not sick; hence, only a little over three-fourths of the people have been represented. And, furthermore, this will put a stop to members staying away for the purpose of blinding their constituents in regard to how they vote.

No. 19. The object of this change is to cause any unrepresented people to immediately obtain representation.

No. 20. The object of this change is to compel strict obedience to the provisions of this Constitution.

No. 21. The object here is to make known to the World, especially the constituents of the Government of the United States, all that takes place in Congress, especially as to who and how each member votes on a question of importance, then their constituents will know whether to send them back or not.

No. 22. The object in this clause is to have men in Congress who know what the word labor means, from not only its Greek root, but by the virtue of experience. Men who don't know what work is are not qualified to represent the bone and muscle of this land.

No. 23. The material change here is to compel all members to vote on all questions; therefore all the people will be represented; will also know how each member votes. As all Representatives are elected by the people; and that the people expect them to go and represent them on all questions, it is their duty to vote for or against all questions. To illustrate the necessity of enforcing this provision : Suppose that the aristocracy had a bill in Congress, and that some members would not vote, and by their not voting against the aristocratic bill they would vote for it; therefore you see the point.

No. 24. This is to make an impression on all conscientious men; for it is the duty of Congressmen to do exactly right; hence none can object to taking this oath.

No. 26. This clause is to prevent Congressmen from leaving the assembly, then going home to canvass their distrct for re-election.

No. 29. This clause is for the purpose of having the salary of public officers increase and decrease, according to the increase and decrease of Labor's salary. The reason for making the amount fifteen times greater is: to qualify one to fill the position, requires a great amount of time and study; hence, such a man should receive more for his labor, on account of having spent so much time in preparing himself for the position. Calculating fourteen dollars per month, $168. per year for farm hands. The present salary of Congressmen which is $5,000, and is twenty-nine and one sixth times greater than the present wages paid to labor. And according to the rate of fifteen times greater, they will receive $2,520, with the exception of the President of the Senate, and Speaker of the House of Representatives, which will receive $4,200. whereas, heretofore they have been getting $8,000. which is equal to forty-seven and thirteen twenty first times greater than the present wages paid to labor. I presume this needs no further argument.

No. 31. This clause carries conviction in its own language, without argument; but I will add a few lines in defense. First, it puts a stop to the introduction of bills, which are without a ray of hope. Second, it puts a stop to the killing of bills in the Committee room, by a Committee appointed by the dominant faction of the assembly. Third, it serves as a test of the politics of members, by compelling them to vote for or against all bills. Then the people will know who they are voting for, and what he will do, judging the future by the past.

No. 33. This provision will probably cause a great controversy. And now we will examine its merits or demerits, either of which you may choose to call. First, it prevents the aristocracy of the Senate, from vetoing the will of the peoples' nearest friends, to wit, the House of Representatives. Second, it prevents the President from vetoing the almost direct will of the people; and gives to the Representatives, that respect and dignity naturally due them. Third, it makes it impossible for the President to rule the people regardless of their wish, and makes each man more of a sovereign than ever before. Who will be the man to raise a dissenting voice or action to this provision? Let him rise in his imbecile proportions, and with his sophistry, defend his perilous position, which will prove more deceiving than building on sand.

No. 36. This clause is to prevent the collection of more revenue than necessary for the expenditures of the Government economically administered. Here I refrain from pages of argument which might be added.

No. 37. This clause compels Congress to levy a tax on the aristocratic indulgences. Also, gives a command, that Congress shall levy a graduated income and land tax. This being the only equitable taxation, that was ever instituted by man; so conceded by all true writers on political economy. Also, this provision exposes all property to taxation. It is just because all property will bring a man an income if he will rightly handle it; therefore he should be compelled to pay a tax on all property.

No. 40. This clause prohibits Congress from borrowing money from any individual or power, until they have issued a full legal tender currency to the amount of sixty dollars per capita. This is nothing more than the duty of Congress in providing for the common defense.

No. 42. This clause declares its object, and if carried out, it will prevent untold crimes, which are being committed every day of every year.

No. 45. This clause is a compromise between two extremes, and as you are aware, that this Constitution is not yet binding, don't be scared. This is the clause which will bring forth controversy, and will make the usury gatherers curse. It will make money plenty, with volume steady; thereby make the prices of labor and its products unvarying, except the slight changes made by supply and demand, which will be temporary, and not a continual decrease of Labor's prices, regardless of supply and demand as it has been since 1866. In 1866 the people had a circulating medium in the hands of the people to about $2,000,000,000. Today according to the World Almanac, the total of money in the United States is $2,092,601,153. But where is all this money, is it in the hands of the people? No Sir, the same report of the Secretary of the Treasury, states that $712,184,062. are in the Treasury of the United States, also states that $318,031,287. are held in National Banks, this giving a total of $1,030,215,349, which are hoarded from circulation in the Treasury and in National Banks alone; now take about $300,000,000, held by other banks; leaving the people about ten dollars per capita. In 1866 the people had $50 perapita. The money was for about two years rapidly drawn from circulation by the shylock legislation, through the infernal bond system; and since then there has been a gradual decrease of the circulating medium by hoarding in the Treasury. This process of contraction has made money dear; hence, labor has been made cheap; interest has become harder to pay; the profit of labor has decreased, while the profits of the creditor class have increased; and labor always being the debtor class, while MONEY POWER is the creditor class. Therefore, you can see that by legislation the MONEY POWER has been especially favored, and that by legislation labor has been, and is to-day especially damned. Furthermore, you can see that, when this provision goes into force, the volume of money will remain the same; that no advantage will be granted to either of the two classes; and, that both classes will be in possession of their moral rights.

No. 46. The simple and plain reason for this provision is that all money should be equal—not have one kind of money redeemable with another kind, but let every dollar be on an equal basis; and the motto of a government should be: To have all money made of the same material, and that the material should be as cheap as possible, for to have a dear money, it costs the people a sum equal to the amount of dearness; and, inasmuch as the legal value of all money is an obligation of a government, in which said government agrees to pay all such obligations; and it is the duty of all governments, as well as an individual, to meet all JUST demands which they have rightfully contracted; then should any independent nation make a contract in constitutionally and rightfully promoting the general welfare, it should meet all such obligations; and, furthermore, should any such independent nation afterward become a province to any other nation, or revolutionize, its just obligations become no more impaired, and the constituents of all such conquered and revolutionized nation should pay their honest debts, for the same reason individuals should pay their honest debts—because they owe them. Hence, the cheaper a money is, the better it is; and the more convenient, the better still; and, as one kind is as good as another, from a legal standpoint. Therefore, the cheapest and more convenient money is best money for the people; and all governments should adopt the best plans. Again, as this provision forbids the issuing of any kind of bonds to maintain a forty dollar per capita circulation; and, as this idea has never been practiced, you may think it too absurd for your attention; but I entreat you to notice the import of the following lines: First, you are aware that a bond is a written promise, made under seal, to pay a certain sum of money, at a certain time, with a certain rate of interest. And, you are also aware that Treasury notes, (paper currency,) is a demand upon the treasury of the government, wherein said government agrees to pay face value of any of its notes.

Now, you know that all government bonds and notes are issued by governments. You know that as long as the contractors exist, they are bound to pay all their bonds and notes, but not bound to pay no more nor less than their face value. You, also know that a bond is no better, nor no worse than a note, that is, in an intrinsic sense. Again, you know that government bonds and notes are both obligations of said government, in which it agrees to pay their face value. Now, considering these foregoing propositions. I call your attention to the reason why these obligations are issued. First, bonds are issued to obtain money, without increasing the circulation. Bonds call for an interest bearing debt. Bonds call for money, and should obtain it; also, they bind a government to pay as much money as they obtain, with interest thereon, until paid: this is the true meaning of bonds. But this was not the purpose of the bonds issued in our last Civil War. They were issued for the purpose of legally stealing the circulating medium from the people; and the design was carried out to the utter destruction of all innocent, and honest business managers. Bonds have been issued heretofore, and claimed to be for the purpose of making the money of the government good. However, the claim has been a delusion; furthermore, it has proved to be a scheme to rob honest labor; and is a lie from title to end.. I ask in the name of reason: how can an obligation of any kind, enhance or maintain the value of a similar obligation? No Sir, the plan hitherto used in issuing of bonds, does not, never did, nor never will enhance or maintain the value of money in the eyes of reason.

In fact, the issuing of bonds in time of war, and then not sell them till after the war is over, also during said war issue a large amount of paper currency with which to pay the debts of a government; then when the war was over retire the money, (steal it,) from the people, after the people have earned it, and need all they have got, then burn in bonfires and otherwise destroy the money of the people, and, furthermore, above or below all the damning schemes that were ever perpetrated against mankind, was the creation of an interest-bearing debt against the people, thereby compelling the people to pay AGAIN the same amount of money that they paid ONCE BY THEIR SERVICES IN THE CIVIL WAR, together with a premium and interest from date till paid. To do all this is more criminal than cold-blooded murder or treason. Yes, I repeat! He who willfully committed such is guilty of crime more heinous than deliberate murder, or treason against blind justice! Of all this the Government of the United States is guilty; done in malice aforethought, or in innocence and carelessness; or, done with both, which is probably the case. All this has been done, and it is claimed to be a correct interpretation of our Constitution.

No. 47. Now, you read a provision which contains an edict against an institution (money power's plausible stealing process, to-wit., National Banks,) and said institution has been and is being applauded as the essence of justice, policy and principle; also, it has been and is to day condemned as unjust and impolitic, and unconstitutional. The latter proposition I affirm and shalll in a brief way attempt to argue. In the first place it is unjust: For the reason that it places a controlling volume of the people's money into the banks, at the power of the aristocracy, subject to the ambition and cupidity of a class of existing mortal men, who are as inhuman as the Shylocks of old. Although civilization forbids their taking a "pound of flesh" nearest the heart, the "law" gives them the absolute right, with immunity, to exact from honest labor a sufficient amount of labor's just reward to satiate that avaricious and natural desire of aristocracy.

The National Banking system places the money, which should be in the hands of the whole people, in the hands of a few privileged individuals. Said system is granted the right to increase or decrease the volume of money at will; thereby increasing and decreasing the prices of labor and the products of labor; hence placing "honest labor" that worthy, and noble calling, and essential prop to national prosperity, on a quicksand foundation. And this mode of proceedure destroys honesty, and inculcates a disposition of hipocrisy; forces the people into an artificial state, soon to fall into the clutches of an absolute despotic money power and be subjected to tyranny of the darkest hue. Therefore, the system is impolitic, and should be annulled, and its direful effects held to the World, serving to arrouse the disdain of wise and patriotic men, that may live in the future; and may its advocates, and their plausible arguments be consigned to the labyrinths of oblivion.

The system is unconstitutional, for the reason: that the Preamble of the Constitution, states in its second provision, that it is for the purpose of establishing justice. Now, the system is granting to a few a monopoly of a power, which should belong to the whole people. The money is the life's blood of a nation's prosperity, to a great degree, and serves the same function to a nation's civilization and prosperity, that blood does to the physical body. The blood of a body being good, the health is good; also, the the blood being impure, the health is virtually destroyed until the impurities are cleansed therefrom. Hence, the money of a nation being inferior, business is stagnated, peace and prosperity gives place to halls of sedition, strikes, lockouts, and starvation.

And when the people would thrive and strike a blow for liberty. this system exerts its power, it stops the circultion of blood in the strong arm of Independence, paralizes Liberty's defense, and administers the drug that produces the deadly stupor of inaction and servility, until the would be actor is bound in the chains of tyranny, while hugging and praising the delusive phantom of hope. Now listen to the language of Andrew Jackson, that old patriot who loved his country, and served it the best he knew how: "Every act of Congress, therefore, which attempts, by grants of monopoly, or sale of exclusive privileges, for a

—50—

limited time, or or for a time without limit, to restrict or extinguish its own discretion in the choice of means to execute its delegated powers, is equivalent to a legislative Amendment of the Constitution, and is palpably unconstitutional."

Who could write in English language, an expression more emphatic and retain such power of logic, than the foregoing. I request you to read the words again, then ask yourself: who is he, that is so dull of comprehension, that he cannot perceive the unconstitutionality of the National Banking System?

No. 48. This provision is nothing more than a correct definition of the term treason. And the definition is no deviation from the rule of judging what is treason. To prove this, you are aware that treason, in the United States, is the levying of war against the United States, or adhering to its enemies, giving them aid or comfort. Now comes the question: who is an enemy of the United States? In answer: it is the man who does, or attempts to vitiate the solemn decrees or obligations of the United States, by a forcible overt action. Now I ask: is not an United States Treasury note a solemn decree and obligation? Yes it is a decree, for each note, on its face, says: the Treasury of the United States, will pay the bearer one dollar or five, as the case may be. Then you see that, he who does, or attempts to depreciate, or buys or sells an United States Treasury note for less than one dollar, is guilty of a forcible overt action against the sovereignty of the United States. It is forcible, because no one will take less than the face value; unless he is compelled; hence, who compels another to take or receives such a note for less than face value, is an enemy of the United States; therefore, by the forcible overt action is guilty of treason.

No. 56. The necessity of this provision is self-evident. It provides against too large a circulation of money; also, against withdrawing the money all at once; thereby, creating a financial crash. All this should be carefully guarded against by human governments, for reasons too evident to need further argument. This provision, also provides against the perpetuation of a National Debt; also, it provides against demanding a premium of the Government, on its bonds.

No. 65. This provision gives occasion to a subject which is controverted very much. The main argument against it is: that God made the world for everyone. Now, admitting that He did, He never gave any man an exclusive right, unless the man earned said right by rightful means. The world does not owe any man a living unless he earns it. Man, with all his rights, has not got the right to be aggressive on the natural rights of other men. No man has a moral right to take a match which belongs to himself and set fire to another's property. No man has a moral right to use his property, or force, for the purpose of destroying another's property or force, except in self defense. Every man is morally bound to preserve himself and posterity from all harm. Then, fellow beings of America, are we not bound to protect ourselves against the invasion of any kind of foreign foe which is hostile to our prosperity? No one can earn a right to kill another, though he work a life-time. Now, here you may say that we can't earn a right to forbid foreign intrusion when the circumstances demand the decree. You may say that if we forbid the pauper labor of foreign countries to land on our shores, or come within our border, we by so doing refuse to let them earn a subsistence, and thereby kill them. But are we duty bound to disregard our own welfare and open our ports for the dregs of all creation? Are we to pay a boon for the victims of tyranny, from every nation of this world? Are we to suffer for the crimes of other nations, and must the penalty be our own destruction? If this is the case, it is right for you to suffer for my crimes; for you to pay my debts; for you to die, that I might live; for you to despair, while I prosper. But, NO! thank Heaven, it is not the case! It is not right for us to suffer for the crimes of foreign nations, by supporting the victims to their greed. No! it is enough to endure the anguish and pain caused by our own mistakes.

No. 75. This provision is one of vital importance, in my estimation, to the future peace of the people. By this provision we will secure the direct will of the people, through a popular vote. Now, I shall not occupy space giving you my opinions and arguments; but I will give you the views of Andrew Jackson on this subject. I now have before me a book containing the Presidents' messages, from George Washington to Tyler's inaugural address; in which I find the following lines in one of Jackson's messages: "I felt it to be my duty in the first message which I communicated to Congress, to urge upon its attention the propriety of amending that part of the Constitution which provides for the election of the President and the Vice-President of the United States. The leading object which I had in view was the adoption of some provision which would secure to the people the performance of this high duty, WITHOUT ANY INTERMEDIATE AGENCY." This is only one of six similar recommendations which he made to Congress. He made the recommendation in nearly every message he made to Congress; and still Congress failed to act. But to-day the idea is becoming prevalent, and it being the exact letter of justice; hence I make this provision. But you may say that Jackson had reference only to the mode of electing by the House of Representatives, and not to the electoral college. However, you will please notice the words, "without ANY intermediate agency." These words mean: the utter exclusion of anything that interferes with the direct vote of the people. No sane man will otherwise interpret the meaning of such invariable words.

No. 76. This is another provision of equal import to No. 75. This provision may seem to some as repugnant to the patriotic spirit of George Washington; but I now quote the words of George Washington, as they appear in his Farewell Address: "The acceptance of, and continuance hitherto in, the office to which your suffrages have twice called me, have been a uniform sacrifice of inclination to the opinion of duty, and to a deference for what appeared to be your desire. I constantly hoped that it would have been much earlier in my power, consistently with motives which I was not able to disregard, to return to that retirement from which I had been reluctantly drawn. The strength of my inclination to do this, previous to the last election, had even led me to the preparation of an address to declare it to you; but mature reflection on the then perplexed and critical posture of our affairs with foreign nations, and the unanimous advice of persons entitled to my confidence, impelled me to abandon the idea. I rejoice that the state of your concerns, external as well as internal, no longer renders the pursuit of inclination incompatible with the sentiment of duty, or propriety; and am **persuaded**, whatever partiality may be retained for my services, that, in the present circum**stances** of our country, you will not disapprove my determination to retire." Now, then, you see that it was not the will of George Washington to serve a second term; but, on account of foreign affairs, and he being a good general and having obtained the confindence of the people, his wise friends gained his consent to serve a second term; and then, in case of war, he would be commander-in-chief of the army of the United States by the virtue of his office. Indeed, it was wisdom at that time; but that time has passed, never to return, and the necessity having ceased, the law should cease. This, none dares dispute. But, the idea of changing the Constitution, and rendering all men inelligible to the second term, did not cease to exist when that old patriot was laid in the tomb. No, but that noble, outspoken Jackson recommended in his messages six times similar language to the following: "I trust that I may be also pardoned for renewing the recommendation I have so often submitted to your attention, in regard to the mode of electing the President and Vice-President of the United States. All the reflection I have been able to bestow upon the subject, increses my conviction that the best interests of the country will be promoted by the adoption of some plan which will secure, in all contingencies, that important right of sovereignty to the DIRECT control of the people. Could this be attained, and the terms of those officers be LIMITED to a SINGLE PERIOD of either four or six years, I think our liberties would possess an additional safeguard." This was Jackson's motto, from first to last, though he was elected to the second term. But Jackson did not speak as emphatic as did William H. Harrison, when he spoke in his inaugural address, in regard to the subject; he made use of the following language: "Until an amendment of the Constitution can be effected, public opinion may secure the desired object. I give my aid to it by ewing the pledge heretofore given, that, under no circumstances, will I consent to SERVE a SECOND TERM." Mr. Harrison gave some strong arguments in defending his position; and the following is a short sketch: "And, surely nothing is more likely to produce such a state of mind, (love of power,) than the long continuance of an office of HIGH TRUST. Nothing can be more corrupting, nothing more destructive of all those noble feelings which belong to the character of a devoted republican patriot. When this corrupting passion, (love of power,) once takes possession of the human mind, like the LOVE of GOLD, it becomes insatiable. It is the never-dying worm in his bosom, grows with his growth, and strengthens with the decling years of its victim. If this is true, it is the part of wisdom for a republic to LIMIT the service of that officer, at least, to whom she has entrusted the management of her foreign relations, the executive of her laws, and the command of her armies and navies, to a period so short as to prevent his forgetting that he is the accountable agent, not principal—the servant, not the master." This old lover of liberty failed to live and carry out this noble idea; however, may his sayings remain immortal. I refrain from further adding arguments on this subject, and thus presuming on your ignorance. I trust that you can understand, without the use of a sledge.

No. 77. This provision is, also, self-evident and argues its own case. However, I refer to the argument made on No. 29. Now, I will show how much the President will receive at this rate: Counting $168 per year for farm hands, it will amount to $21,000. This is a sufficient amount, and I need not to argue.

THE REASONS WHY I OFFER A NEW CONSTITUTION.

"If you dam up the river of progress,
 At your peril and cost let it be!
That river must seaward despite you;
 'Twill break down dams and be free!

"And we heed not the pit-fall barriers,
 That you in its way have downcast,
For your efforts but add to the torrent,
 Whose flood must overwhelm you at last!

"For our banner is raised and unfurled;
At your head our defiance is hurled;
 Our hope is the hope of the ages,
 Our cause is the cause of the world."
C. Nesbitt.

I make no apology for offering this little volume to the public, thereby adding one more to the multiplicity of reform books. I ask no pardon for doing that which I think is a duty I owe to my country. The reason why I offer this Constitution is: That the constitution of a country is the fundamental law of a country, and is subject to the interpretation of men who are authorized to legislate for the people; and all men are subject to human nature, and human nature is not a safe guardian for the liberties of man, when it is surrounded by the various temptations which tend to excite and satiate that "love for money." Therefore, I wish to prove the necessity of making all Constitution a complete interpretation of

—57—

its own provisions; so that no man can interpret and subvert the principles established by the founders of constitutions.

I do not pretend to think that our forefathers, in Constitutional Convention assembled, had any other idea than to promote the general welfare, and make the provisions of this proposed Constitution, a shield to the natural rights of mankind, and serve to maintain the objects set forth in its Preamble, and to debar any infringements on the rights of its subjects by any intriguing force whatsoever, throughout the perpetuity of this proposed Constitution. But were the old patriots—George Washington, John Adams, Thomas Jefferson, Benjamin Franklin, Patrick Henry, etc.—were they here to view our statute books and the present existing condition, which are the result of the interpretation of the Constitution of the United States, they would perceive, in an extreme degree of consternation and instantly, their sad, very sad mistake, and would immediately seek to remedy the existing evils and rectify the past, with that undaunted patriotism shown by them in contending for the natural rights of the "Thirteen Colonies." They would stand up in all their manhood, and with their eloquence, wisdom, physical strength, courage, and military accomplishments, they would strive to overthrow the tyrannical MONEY POWER of the United States, with that degree of independence and determination which they manifested when they declared and fought for their independence, and freed themselves from the despotic rule of that bold usurper, King George III.

Now, I wish to remark, that we should not think that the Old Constitution is too sacred to be changed. It has been changed and enlarged and whole sections rendered, by the Supreme

Court as contrary to the Preamble. As regards its sacredness, there surely can be nothing more sacred to the people of the United States, excepting the Bible, than the Articles of Confederation, which were the basic rules of the Thirteen Colonies while our ancestors gained their freedom from the direct power of Great Britain. What is more sacred in the sense of government, than liberty? Nothing, no, nothing! And when a constitution fails to grant me the rights to which I am entitled, then, right then, its sacredness fades like real landscape views before the omnipotence of the Goddess of Night, to be remembered in future from the fancies of the past, by the good they accomplished, and failed to accomplish.

Are you "conservative," and dare to hesitate in changing a code of laws established by the free will and wisdom of your venerable, worshipped and worthy ancestors? If you are, why are you? Suppose our forefathers of 1776 and their posterity had have been conservative? Do you rely on the present Constitution, because there are a few in Congress to interpret according to the spirit of our forefathers? If you do, why do you? Suppose our forefathers and their posetrity had have relied on the Constitution of England, because William Pitt and a few friends remained in Parliament. What would have been their fate and our destiny? Would we have been free and independent people, with a government of our own? No, Sir, never; we would have been, be, and continue to be subjects to the crown of England, regardless of any acts of despotism enacted or that would be enacted!

Will you dare to point to the actions of the old patriots, who are dead and gone, and with a snear cry "treason?" Will you dare attempt to attaint their worthy and unsullied characters? Will you?

Dare you? I demand an answer— No, no! I dare say you won't; but if you rely on a few friends in Congress, and DEFEND CONSERVATISM, you do it, yes, yes! I aver, and your actions prove the ignoble action. If you are guilty, "repent in sackcloth and ashes," and serve your manhood, and not the vices that have doomed many a lover of LIBERTY to a life of slavery to the assumed LORDS OF CREATION.

The proposition which I have conceived and intend to maintain, is: *That a deficiency in the present Constitution is the cause of the unjust laws, which are written on our statute books and obligatory upon the people of the United States.* Why? Just from the simple fact that the Constitution has given the legislators of the past and present the power to say what was the intention of its founders. Had the present Constitution have specified how it should be interpreted, and stated with that determination and patriotism which its founders possessed, it would have thwarted all attempts of cupidity—that dagger which has let the life's blood flow from BLIND JUSTICE more than once. But now you may ask, why it was not framed in this manner. Well, you are aware of the fact that such a system of government was a new thing to the history of the world, and they did not know what demands would devolve upon such a government. They were warned from every part of the world that such a government would not stand. It was fought by some of its intended constituents. It was fought by all the enemies of LIBERTY, and by some of the ardent lovers of liberty. In fact, it was a little boat at sea, without a compass; but it was piloted by that indomitable spirit of JUSTICE at all hazards.

It has held the confidence of its subjects through nearly all the dangers incident to government. It has gone through foreign invasion, insurrection, civil war, adversity and prosperity, until to-day it stands at the head of all governments, with a population of over 65,000,000 of subjects, instead of 3,000,000, with more wealth than any nation of the globe.

The founders of our present Constitution did not know the demands upon such a government, during periods of peace, war, adversity and prosperity; but the sad experience of the past has demonstrated what we should do, and demands that we should profit by the result of experience. Will you do it? or will you stand in your own light, be a stumbling block in the way of those who would, and doom yourselves, your posterity and your country to the fate that has befallen so many unfortunate nations? Again, will you dare to ignore the sixth or last object of the Preamble of your Constitution? Furthermore, will you willfully disregard the fifth article of the old Constitution? No, no! I trust that you will not. It would be enough to make the most hardened criminal blush to confess such a determination.

The illustrious framers of the old Constitution, with that foresight incident to wise and patriotic men, made a provision, rendering that immortal document capable of being changed, and, thereby, admitting that it was not perfect; therefore, it is NOT our bounden duty to ourselves, with reverence for their service and wisdom, to maintain and perpetuate, unaltered, the provisions contained therein. But it is our duty, according to their declared wish, to alter and change to suit our necessities, in serving the Goddess of Liberty, at whose shrine they bowed in humble adoration.

I know that some will cry, sacrilege, and say that there is no need for a New Constitution. But assertions in a heat of passion, through indignation, prove nothing. And many men have died, and never knew what killed them; many skillful physicians have lost their patients, because they treated for the wrong disease; many men have lost their fortunes through their own conceit; many nations have gone down for lack of proper actions. Such is the nature of man. And, alas! should I receive any condemnation, I will find consolation in this self-evident fact.

This is a progressive world. Will you stop and be trampled underfoot? The manufacturers have thrown aside the plans of our ancestors.
The farmers have laid down the spade and wooden plows, which George Washington used.
In fact the whole industrial system has been changed. Why did not they remain "conservative"? O vain world! Why did you depart from the "ways and means" that our beloved forefath-
pted, why, O why? You all know why.
know that they were compelled to, so, as to compete with the Genius of the World.

I do not think, that this proposed Constitution will be adopted. I only hope to cause investigation of our Constitution; and thereby cause my people to educate themselves in regard to the fundamental principles which should be embodied in our Constitution. Then my mission will be accomplished. And should the present Constitution remain unchanged, I trust that the iniquitous past will pe rectified.

THE SOPHISTRY OF THE MONEY POWER.

Sophist, is a word applied to Greece's seven sages;
Meaning, a wise and clever man for ages,
Until the time of Socrates, Plato, and Xenophon,
Who, with true philosophy, refuted the deception.
Sophistry, today is applauded as true wisdom;
Who will be the men to bind in shackles, this demon;
Who will bid defiance to all deceit;
And fight it with the might of right, destroy in retreat?

Now kind reader I will undertake to refute some of the prevailing deception of modern times in a brief manner, with emphasis. I will take for my criterion, the rule of justice between man and man, subject and crown. Sophistry meant, in ancient times, the same that the word wisdom now means. Sophistry, according to Webster, means: "reasoning in a fallacious, but plausible manner." And in the sense which I use the word; I mean: the deceit that is practiced by politicians. In which they offer, In a plausible manner, some plan of government, claimig that it is justice between subject and crown; and in reality it is: a verry large "campaign lie," designed to deceive, elect, and enslave. Sophists, mean the men who use sophistry; and the men who use sophistry, are men who are so unpatriotic that they sink their own government; men who are ambitious and unjust; men who know better, but want to be counted in the ranks of the dominant and popular party; men who prefer momentary pleasure to a perpetual bliss; men who love their PET PARTY better than they love their wives, children, and best girls, regardless of RIGHT. These are the men that are a bane to the progress of civilization.

Are you one of these kind of men; do any of these shoes fit you? It so, put it on, and prepare to hear your own just condemnation : "Therefore to him that knoweth to do good, and doeth it not, to him it is sin " *James*, 4: 17. Do you defend any of the following deceptive propositions : First. "Conservative reform." Second. "The United States had too much much money in 1866." Third. "We have the best banking system the world ever knew." Fourth. "That tariff reform is all that the farmer needs." Fifth. "That more protective tariff is all that the farmer needs. "Sixth. "That the lack of household and farm economy and industry is all that is wrong with the people." Seventh. "That trusts and combines are all that are injurious to the farmers." Eighth. "That the money lords have a moral right to use their money as they please." Ninth. "That our present condition is not the result of class legislation." Here I might enumerate about 300, which I now have before me, in the first annual report of the Commissioner of Labor of 1886, but I will not.

> He who is conservative,
> Of right, takes the negative;
> He who his country would serve,
> Would conform to right. and never swerve;
> And the principle of right is the same,
> Though parties change their name.

I now begin to give you my views of the foregoing propositions in their order, according to number.

First. "Conservative Reform" is a very common expression by both speakers and writers of either the Democratic or Republican party. It is an admission that there is something wrong; but insists that we continue to remain wrong. It means, be quiet, let my party, (either or both of the Republican and Democratic parties,) reform the present existing evils. It means about as absurd an expression as "Let the Devil reform the wickedness of the world." It means let the Devils "reform," but make the "form" a worse form than the first; and let the "re" push the people into the Pacific Ocean. It means "Let the parties which are led by the aristocracy of this land, continue to rob the lower millions by 'class legislation.'"

It means all this and more— Why does it? you may ask. This is why: First, "conservation," according to Webster, means, to maintain existing institutions; and "reform" means to change; especially from a bad to a good state. Hence you see that each word destroys the force of the other; and it is a meaningless expression. Therefore it is intended to deceive by making a pretense to mean something and meaning nothing.

Then, all deceit has an object. What is its object in this instance? You know that deception means nothing that is good, but invariably means something bad; because, to deceive, you are compelled to lie, and to lie is SIN.

> All through modern and dark ages,
> It has been the cry of sages:
> Ye lords, whom the people have sent
> To legislative halls, while you represent,
> Give us a good money, with volume steady,
> Or for your dying hour make ready
> By repenting in "sackcloth and ashes,"
> For the misery you caused in business crashes.

Second. "That the United States had too much money in 1866." This is the cry of the "poll parrots" trying to imitate that arch villain, Hugh McCulloch, who carried out and approved of the hellish scheme of contracting the currency. It means: "Don't let the lower millions conceive the truth, that the contraction of the currency is one great cause of our national woe." It means to put a break on the prevalent and correct idea that we need more money. It means to insinuate that if we were given any more money, it would become worthless. It means to compel the people to writhe in their agonies, from the extraction of the life's blood of commerce, while the bankers and bondholders, vampires of human government, revel in their glory.

It means all this and more. Again you may ask, Why? And in reply, I ask you to look on the pages of history; and on the reports of statisticans; then you will know the reason, for there you will see that despite the destructive and withering influence of the war, that commerce took more rapid strides in progrsss than hitherto to that time; that all industry assumed the cloak of prosperity; and retained said cloak until the accursed scheme of "contraction" was perfected, then industry's appearance was false, though lightly veiled. Then comes the crash of 1873; then the piteous wails of the victims of the contraction policy; then the drunken feast of the hydra headed MONEY POWER.

This was the condition, and the brazen audacity of none dare dispute, for it is conceded by the world. Was it right, then, to cause all this misery, without even a shadow of a plausible reason? No! No! It was not right; but it was right wrong; for the people did not have too much money. Yet they paid the forfeit of thier own folly by bankrupting all honest industry, and still they suffer the evils thereof.

> The banker preys on friends and foes,
> Gets interest (usury) upon what he owes,
> And loves the people, like lovers of old,
> Who loved the people for their gold.

Third. "That we have the best banking system the world ever knew."

This is a cry uttered by the aristocracy of this land, and by those who want to be in vogue with the upper crust, and by those who don't know any better and do not want to know any better. It means to continue with the National banking system. It means, "Give the circulating medium, the life's blood of commerce, into the hands of a few men; so that they can control the prices of the farmers' products." It means, "Give the sharks of humanity a chance at the liberties of man, that they may utterly banish freedom from America." It means "wage slavery" instead of "chattel slavery," by- controlling the price of labor. It means, "a government of the few, by the few and for the few." It means "an ultimate serfdom, and corn crusts and water for the honest labor."

It means all this, and more— You may ask, Why? And the truth is self-evident. All reason sustains the fact, that if the people need money to carry on the commerce of a country, it is the duty of the legislative and executive powers to give the people what they need; and, is positively their duty to have control of all money; and not delegate the most important power to any individual or corporation. Hence, the "banking system" is a humbug; for it gives to a few men (or shylocks) the power which all the people should have. Therefore, it should be rendered null and

and void by statute law—that power which enforced it upon a people.

> "Tariff Reform" is a campaign song,
> And bids the people come along,
> And vote the old parties for relief,
> Because, thief-like, they cry "stop thief,"
> And the masses join the "hue and cry:"
> Vote 'er straight, without a "reason why."

Fourth. "The Tariff Reform is all that the farmer needs."

This is an expression of both the "old parties;" so expressed by the House bill and Senate bill in the 50th Congress. Also, it is an expression of people who are so narrow contracted that they cannot entertain but one idea, don't understand that and don't believe anyone else does, because they can't explain its virtues. It means that there is something wrong, and for you to vote for the men who willfully persist in doing the same wrong. It means the pure, double-distilled essence of deceit. It means a bitter pill, but the directions say "take her." God only knows what else it does mean, I don't. I might enumerate a hundred definitions, and still its complete definition would be greatly abridged. But, considering all it does mean, I hope you don't mean to say that a reduction of five per cent. of the tariff is the remedy for the abnormal state of the country.

Here the demand for space forbids my discussion of the subject; for to do it justice and myself, it itself would require a volume as large as all this.

> "Protection" is the song of a siren,
> That dwells among ruling men;
> The notes are so sweet men go in ecstacy;
> Though philosophy refutes the fallacy.

> But nations are ruined with its iron heel;
> And, alas! though too late, are made to feel
> The power of its centralization,
> Of the wealth of a once free nation.

Fifth. "That more protective tariff is all the farmer needs.

This euphonious word is adopted by the MONEY POWER to deceive the liberty-loving people; and the little "poll parrot" of an office seeker in his eloquence takes advantage of the word's sweet sound, attempts to show its superiority over everything else; he delves into its complicated parts, using technical words and phrases; skipping here and there, until he gets in about two hours' time, then he in stentorious tones yells, Three cheers for "High Protection!" and as all men want protection against evils, they all join in the "chorus," in the headlong rush to ruin. "High protection" and "Tariff reform" have been the cry of people for ages. The people have been arrayed with capitalists, obstinate stupidity, conceited ignorance, honest innocence, tricksters, politicians, pretended statesmen, and part of the clergy on one side, with the same classes on the opposing side, while the MONEY POWER has been constantly, through day and night, sapping liberty's life blood from its almost exhausted veins. Here I stop, to deal with this subject in the future.

> Economy, Economy! in the house and field,
> And the profits, to the Money Power, yield;
> This has been the cry and practice until
> Billions of wealth move at Money Power's will.
> Economy is a remedy for waste and indolence;
> But not against conspiracy and Providence.

Sixth. "That the lack of household and farm economy and industry is all that is wrong with the people."

This is the expression used by many men. To be sure, it is to some extent true; but is not, by any means, all. However, it is used by men who are enjoying some position, that is, supported by "class legislation." It is, also, used by men who are almost as poor as Job's turkey. These deluded fellows illustrate, by the opportunities which have been afforded to them, and they failed to take advantage of their chances. But, a man who is poor and wants riches, and knows what is the matter with him, knows better than to say that the lack of economy and industry is all that is injuring the people. The man who does say this says: Everybody go to work, make more. And the result would be to take less for what you made. How much better off is a man, when he raises twice as much as he ever did, and then takes half the price he got before? He is worse off, for he has gone to twice the expense, and realized no more money, but has come out in debt.

Some fellow will say that if one man, or a thousand, goes to work and raises twice as much, that the extra production will not affect the prices; and I grant that it will not, but that is not the plan; for before you can give relief, every one must doubly exert himself, according to the remedy. And the natural consequence would be to reduce the price about half, under the present ruling powers.

I now leave this question with you, trusting and requesting that you investigate and see if there is not something more than the lack of economy and industry.

"Trusts and combines," a result of human nature,
Should be dealt with, as other vices, by legislature;
Though not give them power, as heretofore,
To exist, exact, robbing more and more;
But, put a veto on their existence
And make the robbers earn a subsistence.

Seventh. "That trusts and combines are all that are injurious to the farmer."

This is another expression that is very common. It is used by people that "strain at a gnat and swallow a camel." It is absolutely absurd, from the simple reason that they are the result of permission, granted to them by our legislators; and such legislators are selected by the people. Then, whom will you abuse? Will you curse trusts and combines, when you yourselves are to blame? Such a man would attempt to punish a man's gun because he committed a crime with said gun.

> The hydra-headed Money Power,
> Seeking whom it may devour,
> Has got a mortgage on the people,
> The Church, and the church steeple.
> It is worshiped by its victims,
> And praised in sacred hymns;
> It is spoken of in profound reverence
> By people who have'nt any sense?

Eight. "That the 'money lords' have a moral right to use their money as they please."

This is an expression frequently used by people of some intelligence, but is not substantiated by common sense. It never is used by any one who has any idea of moral philosophy, except through deception. To grant these despotic princes the privilege of doing as they please, surrenders to them all the liberties guaranteed to us by the Preamble of our Constitution; makes the declaration of our forefathers a lie on its face, wherein they declared, "that all men are created equal; that they are endowed by their Creator with certain inalienable rights; that among these are life, liberty, and the pursuit of happiness."

Now, is life granted to the people, when their means of subsistence are usurped by these assumed lords of creation? Are your liberties granted unto you, when you are subjected to a code of unjust laws? Is it pursuit of happiness when that you are compelled to earn three times more than goes to your share? No, Sir; certainly it is not.

Furthermore, no man has a right to do an injustice to another man; and it makes no difference whether he acts under legal or physical powers, he has no such right, never did, nor never will under the dispensation of a just God.

> The natural result of class legislation
> Is to ruin a nation by centralization.
> All governments have adopted the plan;
> The result has enslaved every honest man;
> For slavery is more than owning a man, as a mule,
> It is submitting to an unjust and despotic rule.

Ninth. "The present is not the result of 'class legislation.'"

This is an assertion made by men who don't understand the legislation of the past thirty years, and by men who don't want to understand; and by men who understand, but do not want any one else to know. These are the men who hug their chains, worship tyrants, love their enemies more than they love their God. Yes, these are of the kind of men who have enslaved all nations, and are to-day fast enslaving the people of the United States.

Are you one of these three classes? If you are, in the name of the God of Heaven, justice, and liberty to yourselves and all posterity, seek to understand, then endeavor to convice your fellow man; until the might of the ballot sends men enough to Congress, who will abrogate and rectify the unjust laws of the past, before the people rise in their might, and the historian writes upon his pages the horrors of a "bloody revolution," the death of noble heros, martyrs to the Goddess of Liberty; the sufferings of the wives and children, while the husband, father and brother are on the deadly battlefield, there fighting for their "liberties," which were usurped by the legislation of the past.

This has been the history of the world: that when governments become too despotic, some brave leader comes to the front, followed by power enough to right the wrongs to some degree, through the instrumentality of an avenging revolution.

In the language of Patrick Henry: "Let me know the worst, that I may abide by it."

THE CONSPIRACY AGAINST THE HONEST LABORERS OF THE WORLD.

Go, will you, into the depth of the archives of the past. View all history, both sacred and profane. See there written plain, the law of human nature. Then I beseech you to profit by the scene which you there behold.

You will there see that a few designing men have conspired against the honest laborer, since the dawn of civilization. You will see the fact demonstrated in the rise and fall of the Egyptian government. I have now before me a prospectus of the history of the world; in which the artist paints the picture of a scene in Ancient Egypt, which I will now attempt to describe, though language fails to do the picture justice. However, I see a large wagon, about 40 feet long, about 10 feet wide, on its 12 massive wheels, bearing a burden of a very large platform, and upon that platform is a huge idol, representing a large, ferocious animal, about 20 feet in length and otherwise heavily proportioned. But that is not all I see: I see upon the front of that weighty structure several strong cords are attached, and dozens of strong men are ahold of the cords, leaning forward as though with all their strength to please the whims of Pharaoah's tyrannical fancy. Is that all? No. I see upon top of that platform a vicious-looking steward, while in his Satanic Majesty's hand he holds a whip about ten feet in length, nor is it hanging pendant by his side, but I see him leaning forward and plying the lash to some unfortunate victim, who is probably about fagged out, while a slave stands behind the steward and holds an umbrella over him to prevent the sun from tanning his skin that holds his hellish heart. I see another steward riding on horse with a whip of similar kind, using it with the assiduity and satanic disposition of the former. And now I see the result of a seeming fatal blow; I see a manly form stretched writhing on the ground, bleeding from probably a mortal wound, while the surgeons stand around trying to restore him able to perform some more drudgery. Here I might relate the condition of honest labor, as recorded in the history of those times; but I won't occupy the space. I leave you to imagine, and, though you conceive it in the most heinous form, you surely cannot exaggerate.

Then what else will you behold in the scene? As you turn through the pages of history over: Chaldea, Assyria, Media, Babylonia, Persia, Greece, Macedonia, Rome; there you will see the same iniquitous, antique tyranny of Old Egypt, in a modified form.

But does the grand panoramic view cease to show the same disposition of man at this period? No, Sir! But civilization has put a quietus on the brutal mode of the carnal demons. And now the "cunning few" have devised a different plan, in which they control the slaves (honest laborers) and make them believe that they are the renowned and boasted freemen of the world; while they continue to serve their masters from sunup till sundown, scarcely making enough to feed, clothe and care for themselves through the sickness and misfortunes that are incident to the human family. This plan of the "cunning few" is as follows: First, they got control of the traitorous eloquence and the press of the land, and through this medium they moulded the public opinion, then secured the nomination of all the men that they could control; then the people walked up to the polls, and with their elective franchise, turned the key that locked the bands of slavery upon them. Of course there are some that will deny the existence of a conspiracy against them. However, the history of the world goes to prove what I have stated to be true; the present surrounding circumstances, corroborate the testimony; and he who dares to dispute this, refutes his own argument (or sophistry,) and refuses to free himself when the power is at his command.

Again, some skeptic will say that I don't know what I am talking about; that I never lived in those days; that I never participated in such a conspiracy; that I am only 23 years of age; that I don't know very much about anything, and for these reasons refuse to believe what I say. Very well; I don't want you to believe me, unless you wish to, and even if you want to believe me, I don't want you to take my word for what I have said; but go and get you a history of the world and read that; then go to some lawyer and get the Revised Statutes of the United States, and read the laws which I shall call to your attention, on another page.

Again, if I never have engaged in a conspiracy against the honest laborers of the United States, I must confess that I myself, with millions of honest laborers, have participated in a conspiracy against the "cunning few." I know, and so do you, that it is natural for man to want his rights; and that it is natural for some men to want more than what is duly theirs. Therefore, any one who has good judgment of human nature cannot conscientiously deny the existence of a conspiracy against the honest labor of the world. Hence, what is your duty? Will you stand still? You who are rich in this world's goods, and jeopardize your children in their life-time; you who are bound in the "thraldom" of "wage slavery," are you "so good" that when you read in the Bible of Christ's Sermon on the Mount, wherein he says, "Resist not evil," then you succumb to your fate, regardless of how cruel it may be, and fall down upon your knees and offer your petition to God, praying Him to give you your daily bread; then get up from that humble attitude, go to work and earn enough in one day to keep you a week, then gratuitously bestow it on some prince of the MONEY POWER? Where, in the name of God, is your Scripture against going into politics, when it is by politics you are "legally" robbed? Christ went into the Temple of Jerusalem, and with a scourge of small cords he drove the money changers out of the Temple.—St. John 11: 15. Do you know the maxim of Benjamin Franklin?— "God helps those who help themselves."

Who are you? what are you? are you a sane man? or, have you got a guardian to dictate what you are to do or say?

THE CONSPIRACY AGAINST THE HONEST LABORERS OF THE UNITED STATES.

>Once we were a people independent;
>Now the "in" is left off, and we are dependent;
>Not dependent on ourselves, as of old,
>But dependent on "king gold."
>We have not bid this lord, defiance,
>Nor even acted with enough self-reliance.
>We have, on congressmen relied,
>And sent them back, because they "lied,"
>Not for any good that they had done,
>But to rob honest labor without knife or gun;
>Until the people of this nation
>Are under the power of class legislation.

In this little volume, I will be as brief as possible. The first thing I call to your attention is, the attempt of the MONEY POWER of Great Britain to keep our forefathers in submission to the Parliament of King George III. You are all aware of the failure. Second, after they had established their freedom, and their independenc was recognized by the great civilized nations of the World; that this same money power, foresaw the result of freedom of the press, speech, and conscience. Hence, again in 1812, they tried to conquer the spirit or liberty; but only added fuel to the unquenchable flames of independence, that then raged with dominance. Then the tyrants conceived the idea, that what they had failed to accomplish by force, they could accomplish with stealth. So the first thing in order to carry out this hellish design, was to send their agents to our shores, with their money, and shrewd intelligence combined with our own traitors, obtain a majority in our Congress, and then legislate the liberties from the honest laborers of the United States. Second. So as to add speed to their shylock game, they resorted to the old plan of creating "mutiny in camp," and by this plan have the old patriots come to the front, to be shot down by their fellow-men, and then play sad havoc with everything; and then by the mode of their barbarian ancestors, fasten a "great debt" on the people, then to legally steal the profits of those who survived the deadly battle-field. I declare that the foregoing plan has been successfully carried out; and it does not make any difference, whether, or not, they met in their heavily curtained parlors, and preconcerted this plan, the present existing statute laws positively prove that the plan was carried out, and you cannot dispute it, if you know the law.

How was the plan carried out? On the following pages, I will briefly show how.

After capturing a sufficient number of legislators to put a dead-lock on legislation, and in the meantime created a deadly and revenging enmity between the Northern and Southern States on the question of negro slavery, until half past four o'clock, Friday morning' April 12, 1861, when the first gun was fired by the Southern Confederacy on Fort Sumpter. Then began the preparation of a "Belshazzar feast; and until yet, no Cyrus has appeared, but the "hand writing" is on the wall.

The "Civil War" was declared; and to carry on a war a government must have money, and there being but a very small sum of money in the Treasury, there must be some way of getting money. And then comes the act of July 17, 1861, which read as follows:

"That the Secretary is authorized, whenever he shall deem it expedient, to issue, in exchange for coin or in payment of public dues, treasury

—79—

notes of any of the denominations hereinbefore specified, bearing interest not exceeding 6 per cent. per annum, and payable at any time not exceeding twelve months from date; that the amount of notes so issued shall at no time exceed $20,000,000."

The amount issued under this act being $50,000,000. This amount was paid out and still the war went on. More money was needed; hence the act of Feb. 12, 1862, which read as follows:

"That the Secretary of the Treasury, in addition to the $50,000,000 of notes payable on demand, of denominations not less than $5, authorized by the act of July 17, 1861, is authorized to issue like notes to the amount of $10,000,000."

These notes, $60,000,000, were made a full "legal tender" for all debts with no exception; and for that reason stood at par with gold and ¼ per cent. above gold on account of their convenience. And still the war raged, ever adding in its fury every day, threatening to continue for some time. Hence, the government needed more money with which to prosecute the war. Therefore, then comes the act of Feb. 25, 1862, which was as follows:

"That the Secretary of the Treasury is hereby authorized to issue, on the credit of the United States, one hundred and fifty millions of dollars of United States notes, not bearing interest, payable to bearer at the Treasury of the United States, and of such denominations as he may deem expedient not less than five dollars each; *provided*, that fifty millions of said notes shall be in lieu of the demand treasury notes authorized to be issued by the act of July 17, 1861, which said demand notes shall be taken up as rapidly as possible and the notes herein provided for substituted for them; *and provided further*, that the amount of the two kinds of notes together shall at no time exceed the sum of one hundred and fifty millions of dollars, and such notes herein authorized shall be receivable in payment of taxes, internal duties, excises, debts and demands of every kind due to the United States, 'except duties on imports,' and of all claims and demands against the United States of every kind whatever, 'except for interest upon bonds and notes,' which shall be paid in coin, and shall also be a lawful money and a full legal tender in payment of all debts, public and private, within the United States, 'except duties on imports and interest as aforesaid.'"

This act also contained the following section, which now stands on the Revised Statutes of the United States:

"Sec. 3009. All duties upon imports shall be collected in ready money, and shall be paid in coin or in U. S. notes, payable on demand, authorized to be issued prior to Feb. 25th, 1862, and be receivable in payment of public dues.

Act of Feb. 25th, 1862."

Also, the act of July 17, 1861, provided for the issuing of $200,000,000 of bonds; and the act of Feb. 12, 1862, provided for the issue of $500,000,000 of bonds.

Now, why was this exception clause placed on these United States notes, commonly called "greenbacks?" To give a detailed answer, it would take more space than I can afford to occupy; but I refer you to writers who have made the subject a specialty. However, I will briefly make a few propositions, with only enough argument to show you the "design" of the "money power."

In answer to the question, my first proposition is, that, if the exception clause had have been left off of these notes, they would have been worth as much as gold. You may dispute this. However, I will prove it by the "demand notes," (which did not have the exception clause,) standing ¼ per cent. above gold all through the war, even in the darkest hours of peril. And the natural result of the exception clause was to create a demand for gold, with which to pay the duties on imports and interest (usury) on the public debt (fraud). This gave the holders of gold and silver the privilege of demanding two dollars in greenbacks for one in coin; and "there was not to reply; there was but to do or die." The people had to have the coin, on account of the exception clause, (an interpretation of the Constitution); and the bond-holders and bankers, (shylocks,) had most of the coin; and the government, by the exception clause, was gleaning the country for coin to pay the duties on imports, then giving it to the bondholders as interest (usury) on their bonds.

In the meantime these bond-holders were howling "that the government was about to fall;" until in July, 1864, one dollar in gold was worth $2.85 in greenbacks. Notwithstanding that at this date the Union army was the victor of the field ; for according to the history of the war the Union army had cut off the supply of the Southern Confederacy, and had drove them to the wall; had starved the South almost to death; and the North had two men to the South's one; furthermore, the Union army was winning almost every battle, and yet a greenback, (a note against the government, secured by over $15,000,000,000 of wealth,) at this date was only worth .35 5-57 in gold. Hence, the bondholders got $2,844,649,626.69, of United States bonds for about fifty cents on the dollar, making a profit of $1,422,324,313.34, plus $97,772,891.07, of profit by getting their interest (usury) in gold; making a grand total of $1,519,097,204.41; which was legislated into the coffers of the vampire bondholders, at the expense of honest labor, in the short space of five years—enough money to make 1,519 millionaires. And yet this legislative steal is a small one compared with others, and it is abridged.

You may ask, What was a greater legislative steal than this? And I will only briefly answer the question:

The adoption of the interest-bearing bond system was the grandest scheme that the MONEY POWER ever interpolated in the United States Statutes.

However, some of you may think that this was a matter of necessity; but suppose we investigate and see whether it was or not. According to the Constitution, Congress had the right to coin money; and since the war the Supreme Court has decided that Congress had and has the right to issue paper money in time of war, and in time of peace. And then the condition was such that the people needed money. Hence, it was the duty of Congress to issue a sufficient amount of money, based on the wealth of the people, and give it to the people in payment of their service rendered to the government. Then what the government bought with said money, should have been used to sustain the government. And the money should have belonged to the people, for they had dearly paid for the money by their service, and thousands had sacrificed their lives for their country, while the bankers and bondholders assembled in their guild halls, far, far from danger; there bleeding the patriotism of their country, both physically and financially. Then they were titled by many as the "friends of their country"; but, to-day, by honest intelligence and wisdom, they are recognized in the "rogues' gallery" as the fiends of mankind, a worse bane to civilization than Jesse James and his notorious band.

This may shock the solemnity and moral rectitude of some; nevertheless the facts in the case I now submit to prove:

First: while Jesse James only robbed the "people," (railroads and banks,) of their thousands by the force of the revolver; the bankers and bondholders robbed honest labor of billions through legislation. Now you may ask how they got these "billions" by legislation. The answer is simple and plain to an unprejudiced mind, and is as follows: first, the people paid for all money that they received. Second, bonds were issued for every dollar that was issued, said bonds bearing interest, paid semi-annually in gold. Third, the gold and silver sharks, through the appreciation of coin, caused by the "exception clause," bought these bonds for half price, and retired and destroyed the people's money, created a great debt (fraud), left the people with a small amount of money to pay a large interest-debt (fraud); and to-day, in the past, are now and have been paying a debt (fraud), that was "PAID ONCE" on the battlefield, and in support of the government.

To prove that this steal amounts to "billions," I present to you the following table, taken from the reports of the Secretary of the Treasury:

Net Ordinary Receipts of the U. S. during the periods of 1861 and 1862.	Net Ordinary Expenditures. Interest not Included.	Interest.
$ 41,276,299.49	$ 62,616,055.78	$ 4,034,157.30
51,919,261.09	456,379,896.81	13,190,344.84
112,094,945.51	694,004,575.56	24,729,700.62
243,412,971.20	811,283,679.14	53,685,421.69
322,031,158.19	1,217,704,199.28	77,395,090.30
$770,934,634.48	$3,241,988,406.57	$173,034,714.75

Interest, - $173,034,714.75
Total Expenditures, $3,415,023,121.32.
Receipts, - 770,934,635.48
                                    ─────────────
                        $2,645,088,485.84

This table shows a debt of $2,645,88,485.84, but don't include all expenditures. The report of the Secretary of the Treasury shows that the total principal was on August 31, 1865, $2,844,649,626.56.

This report also shows that there was currency issued in all kinds to the amount of $1,996,000,000. This report furthermore shows a statement of the Secretary, stating that for every $100,000,000 paid out of the Treasury, there was $25,000,000 paid out for discount—high price demanded on account of the high price for gold, said high price, the result of the "exception clause," an interpretation of the Constitution.

Therefore, the following table will show the cost of the adoption of the interest-bearing bond system, and the "exception clause:"

Total bonded debt, 1865   — —$2,844,649,626.56
Interest, already paid,   — — 2,410,000,000.00
Interest, yet to be paid, — —   550,000,000.00
Money is'd more than nec'sary—   505,000,000.00
                                 ─────────────
Total steal,   -   -   —$6,309,649,626.56

You will please excuse my saying "total," for I have not given the amount in compound interest, which they have had the privilege of getting; neither have I given the amount of difference between one per cent. and ten per cent. on an average of $300,000,000 for 25 years, which the bankers have enjoyed. I have, probably, said enough to arouse the indignation and curiosity of all true born patriots; enough to cause an investigation.

And now I refer you to writers who make this subject a specialty. See list advertised in this book. To discuss this subject alone is not my object.

The next thing on the list of conspiracy is the National Banking Act of February 25th, 1863. I cannot give space to the many sections which constitute the Act; but will give you its declared, and real objects. First, I will describe the law in brief: It provided, that any number of natural-born persons, not less than five, with a capital of not less than $50,000, shall engage in and enjoy the privileges of the Act. The privileges were: That any capitalist could buy United States notes with their appreciated gold for about fifty cents on the dollar; then buy United States bonds, dollar for dollar, thereby obtaining one dollar of bonds for fifty cents in coin; then they could deposit $100,000 of such bonds with the Treasurer, which they had bought for $50,000; and then the Treasurer would issue $90,000 in Bank notes, for which the bankers had to pay one per cent. interest, being $900. But the government would pay the bankers five per cent. on the $100,000 worth of bonds deposited; and would exempt their bonds and notes from taxation.

Therefore the bankers would make a profit according to the following table:

Amount actually invested,	$50,000
Interest paid on circulation,	900
Total expense,	$50,900
Amount of interest on bonds,	$5,000
" of " on circulation,	9,000
" gained, being exempt from taxation,	1,900
	$15,900

This makes 31 per cent. on their money; beside all this, they loan other people's money, get interest on what they owe and all that they have got invested; and are exempt from taxation. In the meantime they work (or steal) six hours a day, and then say that banking don't pay.

Well, banking don't pay (the people), and they should have their business (stealing) stopped right away.

The declared object was to furnish the government money with which to carry on the war. And you who say that the banks came to the country's rescue, I ask you to look at the Treasurer's reports, during the war. On July 1, 1864—one year, four months and six days from the enactment of the law—there was only $31,235,270 of bank notes in existence; not enough money to bear the expenses of the government a week. That looks like coming to the country's rescue, don't it? But when all danger had passed, then they increased their circulation to its limit. Oh, what patriotism?! They loved their country even unto death, (the death of the country, I mean.)

The real object was to own enough of the circulating medium to control the volume of money; thereby regulate the price of labor and labor's products; hence subject a nation of people to the thralldom of "wage slavery," both "black and white."

The next thing on the list is the contraction law of 1866. I cannot afford to give space to this law, either, although I will give you its object.

In the first place, you are aware of the creation of an enormous debt (fraud); and that the people had about $2,000,000,000 of money, exclusive of the gold and silver, with which to pay the debt, and would have soon paid it, had it not been for the "Contraction Act," which took the money from the people, reduced the price of their products, promoted the bankers to the position of Commander in Chief of MONEY VOLUME. And they knew, full well, their duty; so, that they have so skillfully carried out their task, that the United States debt (fraud) of to-day is as hard to pay, and would take more of the laborers' products to pay it, than it would have taken to pay it in 1866. Notwithstanding, there has been about $4,000,000,000 of principal and interest already paid; and yet the debt (fraud) is as large as ever. This is another assertion that may be controverted, but it will prove itself:

As the tax to pay with must come off of labor's product, suppose we compare the prices of that date with the present. Now, we will take wheat, labor's main resource. The average price of wheat in 1866, according to the American Almanac, was $2.82½ per bushel. The average price of 1889, about .82 per bushel. Hence you can see that it is about 3⅓ times harder to pay a billion dollars now than it was then. The debt (fraud) was then nearly $3,000,000,000; now over $1,500,000,000; therefore, you can see that the debt (fraud) is harder to pay now than it was then.

The real object was to prevent the payment of the STEAL, and fund it into centuries, thereby compel the honest labor to pay tribute to the MONEY POWER forever, or until ——

Now, I refer you to your reason.

The next act is of great import, and is known as the "Credit Strengthening Act;" and reads as follows: Sec. 3693. The faith of the United States, is solemnly pledged to the payment in coin or its equivalent of all the obligatins of the United States, not interest bearing, known as United States notes, and of all the interest bearing obligations of the United States, except in cases where the law authorizing the issue of any such obligations has expressly provided that the same may be paid in lawful money or other currency than gold and silver. But none of the interest bearing obligations not already due shall be redeemed or paid before maturity, unless at such time United States notes are convertible into coin at the option of the holder, or unless at such time bonds of the United States, bearing a lower rate of interest than the bonds to be redeemed can be sold at par in coin. The faith of the United States is also solemnly pledged to make provisions at the earliest practicable period for the redemption of the United States notes in coin. Act of Dec. 18, 1869.

Why was this section of law enacted?

And in answer, I will call your attention to the fact, that there was $346,000,000, of the "greenbacks" that escaped, with a narrow chance, the force of contraction. And the bondholders did not want these "greenbacks" in payment of their bonds, but wanted gold or its equivalent; hence comes the "Credit Strengthening Act," making the debt (legal steal) $675,000,000 larger; also, making it payable in coin; thereby adding this enormous sum to the coffers of the bondholders on account of the premium paid on coin. This being a legislative steal, for the reason, that the bondholder first agreed to take any legal tender money and this included the "greenbacks." Therefore, the object of this law, was to add a few hundred more millionaires to the already existing hundreds that had been legislated into existence.

But, hark! After the foregoing law was enacted, a sound comes from the Nevada silver mines, that quakes the entire shylock kingdom.

The bondholders were not content with coin, unless it was dear; and fearing that coin would become plenty, and then the people could pay their debts; and the creditor classes would cease to reap their annual barest of usury. Hence, comes the Act, demonetizing silver——

Here, I now close my brief sketch of conspiracies. I have only endeavored to call your attentiou to the conspiracies against the honest laborers of the Unitd States; hoping that you will further investigate. I give you a list of books, and admonish you to read and act, or else you will be trampled underfoot by the iron heel of despotism.

WHAT IS WRONG WITH THE PEOPLE OF THE UNITED STATES?

First, it is a medicine which they have been, and are still taking; and a receipt for the compound is as follows: Equal parts of

Avarice. { Love of power. Love of gold. Love of fame. Love of self. Love of nobility, regardless of right.

Indolence, { In National affairs. In State affairs. In County affairs. In home affairs. Trusting to other men's judgment.

Conceit. { Thinking that man is cute, and, that you are wisest. Thinking that all men are fools, and that they will remain fools.

The lack of:
{
Education.
Resolution.
Independence.
Patriotism.
Self reliance.
Knowing how to love one's country.
}

This is a compound that is patented by the Devil, and the people of the United States are good customers. The directions for taking are as follows:

(1.) Get up early and go to work.

(2.) Work hard all day, and don't think of anything else, for fear you get too smart.

(3.) When night comes, go to sleep, if you get a chance, so that you will be able to serve your masters on the next day.

(4.) Serve the MONEY LORDS all the time, every day and every year; because they are such good people; almost got wings? (wings to fly to Hell with.)

(5.) Don't fret nor grumble, everything is all right, but you are all wrong; 'tend to your own business.

(6.) Don't read nor talk, lest you learn, and offend the dignity of some people

(7.) Vote the ticket your father did, and vote it straight, provided you vote for millionaires; they can buy any law that they want?

(8.) Believe what your party bosses say; they are "sages?" and all they want is only some office, then to serve (or steal from) the people.

(9.) Be obedient unto your masters, do what they say, right or wrong; kill and starve, if necessary, or else you will be damned.?

(10.) Comply with these directions; especially teach your children, wives, sisters, brothers, grampas, grandmas, uncles, aunts, nephews, nieces, colonels, captains, corporals, privates, friends and all their friends; in fact do the duty of a slave, and teach the whole world to be obedient to the MONEY POWER.

The natural effect of this medicine is to totally destroy liberty and fraternity, and centralize the wealth of the people into the hands of a few men, and make slaves of the yeomanry of every land. This has been the result in all nations' last days.

The most learned pharmacists of this compound are bankers, bondholders, money brokers, and privileged corporations. The spoon with which they feed their medicine to the patient is: the subsidized press, party bosses, and the scheming intelligence of office seeking, eloquent orators. In reality, the vices of man have placed us in our present condition.

It is the nature of man, for a scheming few to work against the prosperity of the whole, by the means of deception.

I will now quote the language of William H. Harrison, used in his inaugural address:

"It was a remark of a Roman Consul in an early period of that celebrated Republic, that a most striking contrast was observable in the conduct of candidates for offices of power and trust, before and after obtaining them—they seldom carry out in the latter case the pledges and promises made in the former. However, much the world has improved, in many respects, in the lapse of upwards of two thousand years since the remark was made by the virtuous and indignant Roman, I fear that a strict examination of the annals of some of the modern elective governments, would develop similar instances of violated confidence."

Now, you see that deception has been the mode by which designing men have obtained power in human governments. It is a disposition of man to deceive and to be deceived.

All constitutions of human governments heretofore, have given men the right to make good promises to the people before their election, and when elected they are made privileged characters; that is, they can make good laws or bad laws, suiting their own taste about what the Constitution means.

All constitutions have allowed the most aristocratic "demons" to obtain seats in the people's legislative halls. These "demons" have never been known, in history, to grant the masses equitable laws, unless through a concession, when their lives are threatened by the just revenge of an oppressed people.

All constitutions have been bent and twisted to suit the various opinions of each legislative assembly; and each opinion is claimed to be a correct interpretation of the constitution, according to a preamble which declares for exact justice; and the rule of justice is immutable, yet each different, and even the same, political assembly enacts laws *visa versa* to the preceding assemblies! and each assembly claims allegiance to the exact letter and spirit of the framers of their constitution.

All constitutions have been bent and twisted to suit men's views, just like the Bible, until there are 666 denominations of religion, when in fact there should be but one; for there is only one God, one Heaven, one road, one criterion, to which all shall be subjected; also there are now, on account of the various opinions of justice between man and man, hundreds of isms, ics, and ty-ty's, and the men of every land are divided on every hand.

Yet justice has but one throne, one law, one object, and these are plain to all sane men.

, Some people have become infidels and very immoral persons, on account of the various opinions on true religion; also, some people have become Anarchists and Socialists on account of the failure of constitutional governments in granting equitable laws to the people.

This is what is wrong; now comes the "remedy."

THE REMEDY.

First. Agitate until the whole people begin to meditate; and agitate until the whole people educate themselves to know what is wrong, and how to love their country. And when you educate the whole people thus, they will become resolute, independent, self-reliant; then while they are in this stage of action, let them adopt a CONSTITUTION that is the exact letter of justice, and make said Constitution containing provisions adapted to a country in times of war, in times of peace, prosperity, and adversity; and make said Constitution an interpretation of itself. Say what Congress shall do, and what it shall not do. This may be easier said than done; but it must be done before we prosper; and it will be done, I hope, in the near future, if the people want it done; and if they don't want it done, they seal their own doom—this is brief, but it means volumes. Do it, and you brave, despotic tyrants, you will defeat the last resort of designing men, to-wit: unjust legislation. You will make yourselves and all posterity the happy recipients of prosperity, fraternity, liberty and the laws of justice. It is a waste of time; for to make our demands only in statute law, if we wish to effect any permanent good, for the reason that it has taken about 15 years to educate the people to the present stage of action, and still their object is unattained; but should honest labor in the near future get strong enough to obtain their wishes, and only make their demands in statute law, how long would it be till the designing few would get into power, and change the statute laws to suit the taste of the aristocracy? It certainly would not be long. Therefore, our demands must be embodied in our Constitution, and made hard to change, or else in a few years we will have to leave the party name which adopted our demands, and renew the struggle for liberty, in the ranks of a new party; for all reforms are brought about through the instrumentality of a third party. For instance, our forefathers were a third party in the Kingdom of Great Britain. The Republican party was a third party in America to free the negroes from chattle slavery. Now, what will be the name of the new party, which will free the people of the United State, both white and black, from a slavery to the money power?—That new party must come, and come soon, or it may be too late; for never in history did an old party radically reform, and we must have a radical reform.

CONCLUSION.

Kind reader, now I conclude this brief little volume, which I have submitted to your decision. And if you will criticise ; as I am not present to reply, I ask one more favor, to wit, that you will declare to your friends, that condemnation which you deem that I deserve. And if I am guilty of a deviation from the precepts of Justice, I invoke upon myself a penalty equal to the offense. If this little volume will not stand the crucial ordeal of scrutinizing righteous reason, it does not comply with the wishes of its author; and I ask, that its defects be clearly expounded, and made known to the world. Then you may give me the name of one who loves his country, but knows not how to serve that adored object of all true born patriots. But should this volume stand the philosophy of equity, I ask, not for pages of eulogy, nor songs of praise, but I implore you to devote all your spare time and energy in carrying into effect the manifested object of its author. I have only briefly stated and argued my propositions, with the view to invite an investigation of the past, regardless of filial or party ties;

For he who fears to unearth the truth,
Is not a patriot, but a coward, a traitor forsooth.

Will you refuse to investigate, and be stigmatized as a coward and a traitor? If you do, you blight your own happiness, you damn your own selves by such refusal.

Or, will you investigate, and fulfill that noble calling of an honorable man, boy, woman, or girl, who loves their country, and dares to vindicate their natural rights?

I have abridged this volume, so to make it as cheap as possible, that it may reach more readers; that it may be echoed from every hill, prairie and dale; and sent across the Atlantic wave; and that its success or failure will be great; and now come weal or woe, its final words will soon be spoken.

Hark! Have ye brave sons and fair daughters?
Have ye reverence for those who crossed Atlantic Waters?
Look into the future, and behold your sons' and daughters' fate,
And redeem them before the time grows late!

May the good that this volume does be appreciated, and may the God of Mercy forbid its bringing harm on my fellow man, and if the idea is right, may it redeem the long-cherished hopes of all oppressed people of the world, from equator to pole.

History of the Wheel and Farmers' Alliance,
    Large Illustra'd vol., 778 pages, *Morgan*, $2.25
Alliance and Labor Songster, - *Vincent*, .10
Smith's Diagram of Parliamentary Rules, for
    Alliance and Literary, - - .50
The Irrepressible Conflict, - - *Hull*, .15
Tokology, for Woman, cloth, *Dr. Stockham*, 2.00
Prospects for Humanity, 2 Lect's, *Randall*, .15
Your Answer or Your Life, 100 p., - *Hull*, .25
Hazard Circular, - - - - *Heath*, .10
Principles of Moral and Political Economy,
    large paper, 190 pages, - - *Jones*, .50
Baker on Money, standard, - - *Baker*, .25
Pointers, 80 pages, - *Hart and Rhodybeck*, .25
Labor, Capital and Money, - *Camp*, .50
Immortality, 96 pages, - *J. Vincent, Sr.*, .25
Looking Backward, cloth, - *Bellamy*, 1.50
Financial Catechism, 3rd edition, paper,
    332 pages, - - - - *Brice*, .50
Hist. of the Coffeyville DynamitePlot, *Vinc't*, .25
No Interest for Money, - - - *Gibbs*, .25
Hard Times and the Way Out, *Brooks*, } 10
Seven Financial Conspiracies, *Emery*, } 10 .25
Babies and Bread, - - *Houser*, } 10
Perfect Motherhood, cloth, - *Waisbrooker*, 1.50
Papa's Own Girl, paper, *Marie Howland*, .30
Papa's Own Girl, cloth, - " " .45
Speaking of Ellen, paper, - - *Ross*, .50
Whither Are We Drifting? - - *Wiley*, 2.00
National Economist Almanac, - - - .15
The Great Red Dragon or London Money
    Power, cloth, - - - - *Wolfolk*, 1.00
    Reduction:—$6 worth from list for $5 cash.
    Address H. & L. VINCENT, Winfield, Kansas.

CPSIA information can be obtained
at www.ICGtesting.com
Printed in the USA
BVHW04*1221080818
523683BV00043B/350/P